CLASSIC ITALIAN COOKING

for the Vegetarian Gourmet

Dedication:

To our husbands, Gordon and Bill, two discriminating palates who have tasted and approved all these recipes.

CLASSIC ITALIAN COOKING

for the Vegetarian Gourmet

BEVERLY COX
with
DALE WHITESELL

CRESCENT BOOKS
New York • Avenel, New Jersey

Designed by Keith Sheridan Associates, Inc.

Produced by Smallwood & Stewart, 9 West 19th Street, New York, New York 10011.

This 1993 edition published by Crescent Books,
distributed by Outlet Book Company, Inc., a Random House Company,
40 Engelhard Avenue, Avenel, New Jersey 07001.

Printed and bound in the United States of America.

Random House
New York • Toronto • Sydney • Auckland

Library of Congress Catalog Card Number 84-40117

ISBN 0-517-10042-8

8 7 6 5 4 3 2 1

CONTENTS

INTRODUCTION

This book is for people who enjoy good food but want to reduce their consumption of meat. In Italy as well as in North America there is a growing trend toward this kind of healthy and practical cooking. But many people are under the impression that to cook without meat means sacrificing gastronomic pleasure. The recipes that follow will, I hope, show how wrong this is.

The Italian kitchen is blessed with an enormous range of high-quality fruits and vegetables which naturally fortify a meatless diet. From the cooler mountainous regions come wild mushrooms, fennel, hazelnuts, and asparagus (as well as some of Italy's greatest wines). The many orchards produce an abundance of pears, apples, and cherries. In the South, olives, tomatoes, garlic and peppers, artichokes and zucchini, oranges and lemons, melons and almonds flourish in the hotter Mediterranean climate. Italy's range of cheeses is second only to that of France and of course, pastas in seemingly infinite flavors, shapes, and sizes offer an almost unparalleled resource for the creative vegetarian cook.

The Italian cuisine is not one but many; by driving for a few hours through the Italian countryside you will come across entirely different styles of cooking and even the same dish prepared in very different ways. For anyone writing an Italian cookbook this presents a dazzling challenge; for the inventive cook it means each recipe should be just a starting point in exploring the many faces of Italian cooking.

In the 150 or so recipes that follow I have presented a cross-section of this marvellous variety, from minestrones to pesto, risottos to ravioli. Many are traditional; some are completely new. There are dishes here for every occasion, from quick snacks and soups to rich sauces and fresh pastas ideal for a dinner party. The majority of recipes require few special ingredients or complicated or time-consuming preparation.

Italian cooking is justifiably one of the most popular in the world. It has less of the formidable emphasis on rules than does French cooking, yet offers an equally exciting variety of dishes. This book introduces some of those dishes, and I hope that you will get as much pleasure from making and serving them as I have.

CHAPTER 1

THE ITALIAN KITCHEN

ood ingredients are the building blocks of good cooking of any kind. A skillful cook can do a lot to disguise bland vegetables, stale herbs or spices, or a tasteless cheese, but the best cooking begins with fresh, quality foods and lets their flavors speak for themselves. This does not necessarily mean that you must always select the most expensive ingredients; rather, you should shop carefully and critically. Just as all cooking oils (and even all olive oils) do not taste the same or have the same cooking qualities, so all tomatoes are not equal. In the pages that follow I have included a few of my own guidelines for choosing ingredients; use these and follow your own judgment and experience.

Vegetables and Fruits

It is important to keep in mind what fresh ingredients are in season when planning a menu, especially a vegetarian one. Don't be persuaded too easily by glossy tomatoes or salad greens in mid-winter or other out-of-season produce. Very often these have little flavor and have suffered in traveling the long distance to the store. I have attempted in these recipes to use a wide range of winter and summer produce and give dishes that can be adapted according to what is available.

When selecting vegetables or fruits, avoid those that are bruised or mushy; the color should be even and vibrant, skins should be shiny but not greasy, leaves should be crisp. (I never recommend the ubiquitous iceberg lettuce; with Bibb, romaine, Boston, and the rarer radicchio, arugula, escarole, even dandelion leaves, there are plenty of better and tastier alternatives.)

Although many Italian vegetables and fruits were introduced from other countries, it is the Italians who have developed the high quality strains which grace their tables. The tomato is a perfect example. Brought to Italy from the Americas green and small, purely for its decorative qualities, it was cultivated to produce the rich, red Italian plum tomato which is perfect for cooking and especially, eating in salads. Fresh plum tomatoes are available throughout the summer and are preferable to other varieties, but may be substituted by any ripe tomato or good quality canned, whole, peeled plum tomatoes imported from Italy.

Tomato peeling: core the tomatoes and score their skins on the bottom with a small 'x'. Plunge them in batches into boiling water for 20 to 30 seconds. Refresh immediately in cold water. Peel and halve the tomatoes and scoop out their seeds.

Fresh green asparagus has become widely available throughout the United States in spring, when the cooler weather and longer sunlight hours combine to nurture this perennial crop. In Europe, the spears are covered with their sandy soil as soon as their points pierce the earth, producing a thin-skinned white asparagus found here only canned or in specialty shops. The same tender effect is duplicated by peeling off the stalk skins with a vegetable peeler and blanching or steaming the asparagus in salted water.

Eggplant is freshest when its shiny purple skin is unblemished and firm and its pulp is without a hint of green. The smaller variety is tastier but if large eggplant must be used, scoop out the seeds, which have a tendency to be bitter. You may also salt the eggplant after cutting it to extract the bitter juices. Drain on paper towels for 30 minutes, weighting the eggplant down with a cutting board or plate.

Zucchini, called *courgette* by the French and English, is native to Italy. The small ones are the most tender and may even be eaten raw in salads or marinated. The freshest zucchini are firm, neither hard nor spongy, with dark green skins that are evenly mottled and shiny. Although zucchini vary in length from 6 to 10 inches, the tastiest are about 6 to 7 inches in length and about 1½-inches in diameter. If you have any doubt about their freshness, peel thinly to remove their skins; this will eliminate any bitter aftertaste.

Fresh mushrooms are available all year long but should be chosen only when their white caps are tightly closed and unbruised, a sign of freshness. Handle them gently, wiping them with a damp cloth to clean off any dirt or sand. After slicing or quartering, sprinkle with lemon juice to keep them white. And, above all, don't overcook them to a rubbery state. Rather, keep them a little raw in the center, as they will continue to cook for several seconds in the heat of the dish.

Wild mushrooms are the glorious, woodsy-flavored gems which stud the Italian menu in the early summer and fall. The *porcini, faggio,* and *funghi imperiale* are but a few of the woodland mushrooms that add fragrance to the table, and in their dried form permeate Italian dishes throughout the year.

In this country, dried wild mushrooms may be found in Italian groceries or gourmet shops. Although expensive, only a small amount is needed for any dish as they have a very concentrated flavor. Before using they should be steeped in hot water. Reserve the liquid to use in the recipe; if it is gritty, filter through a fine sieve or paper coffee filter.

Frozen vegetables are acceptable substitutes for fresh when absolutely necessary or, as time is often scarce, need permits. Spinach, peas, and artichokes are the most acceptable replacements and should be steamed or boiled just until thawed in most of the recipes. Canned vegetables have usually suffered oversalting or overcooking or both, although food companies are just starting to be more taste and quality conscious in their canned foods. However, better a ripe, canned tomato than a woody, tasteless, mealy fresh one.

Cheeses

Specialty cheese shops are taking advantage of the rapid importation by air to provide a greater range than ever before of Italian cheeses. Parmesan, mozzarella, and ricotta are only the most well-known of the dozens of soft and semi-soft cheeses, goat and sheep cheeses, and hard, grating cheeses (for information on some of these, see Page 210). The only way to judge cheese before buying is to taste the cheese to ensure that its flavor is fully developed without smelling of ammonia, which the soft-ripening cheeses are especially prone to take on when overripe. Look at the rind, which should never be dry or cracked, or show signs of oiliness.

Fresh soft cheeses should be purchased as close as possible to serving, as their condition deteriorates within a matter of days. Harder cheeses last longer if stored properly; wrap the cheese in dampened cheesecloth and refrigerate, dampening the cloth each day until the cheese is used (this allows the cheese to breathe). Or, wrap in aluminum foil and keep cool in the cheese drawer of the refrigerator.

Allow the soft and semi-soft cheeses to come to room temperature for one hour before serving. Harder cheeses require a few hours, depending on the size of the piece and the temperature of your kitchen. Aged cooking cheeses such as parmesan or pecorino romano should be grated fresh for using, either by a small hand grater, blender, or food processor.

Nuts

Nuts of all kinds: almonds, walnuts, hazelnuts, chestnuts, pine nuts (pignoli), and pistachios are used widely in Italian cooking, predominantly in desserts, but also in pesto and cream sauces. They provide a good source of protein, especially when accompanied by grains or dairy products.

Rice

Most of the recipes in this book call for Italian Arborio rice. Grown in the alluvial soil of the Po River Valley, this rice is characterized by its short milky white grain with a pearl drop in the center. It is perfect for the risotto method of cooking, during which slow absorption of liquid softens the grains to a creamy, *al dente* state.

American long grain or Carolina rice may be substituted for Arborio with less successful results in texture and flavor, as they will not absorb as much liquid without turning to a mush. If you cannot use Arborio, reduce the amount of stock so that the desired consistency is obtained.

Flours

Unless otherwise stated, all recipes in this book use unbleached, all-purpose flour. Bread flour, with its higher gluten content, works admirably with the bread and pizza recipes, but it absorbs more liquid. So, with this flour, start out by using less than called for in the recipe and augment, if necessary, when kneading the dough.

Semolina, a hard durum wheat flour, is also high in gluten and protein content and is used to make the imported Italian dry pastas or macaronis. It gives them a golden color and a firmer texture than egg and flour pastas.

Butter and Eggs

I always use unsalted butter as it is sweeter and fresher than salted. All recipes in this book call for large eggs, unless otherwise specified.

Olive Oil

Olive oil is probably the most important staple of the Italian kitchen (only in the richer, northern regions does butter figure as a cooking oil).

For vinaigrettes I recommend nothing but the best, extra virgin olive oil. This is made from the first pressing of hand-picked olives to capture the purest taste and richest color. Oils from Lucca, in Tuscany, are delicate-flavored and golden-green; those from Sicily are deep green with a richer, stronger olive flavor to match the robust cuisine of the island.

For sautéeing, when the flavor of the oil is not so important, you can use the milder, almost odorless 'pure' olive oil—the type that is generally sold in supermarkets—as this has a higher smoking point than extra virgin. All olive oil has a much lower smoking temperature than other vegetable oils, however, and should not be used for deep-frying as its fine flavor is ruined when subjected to high heat over a long period. For deep-frying I recommend using vegetable oil.

Deep-frying: when deep-frying, it is very important that the fat be between 360° and 400°. If you don't have a thermometer, fry a piece of bread in the oil before adding the food. If the bread sits there soaking up oil, continue to heat the oil and test again. If the bread browns in seconds, the oil is too hot. Only when an even golden brown color is achieved after a minute of frying can you be certain that the temperature is right. Wait a few seconds between batches so that the oil has time to reheat to the proper temperature.

Vinegars

One of the most prized vinegars in Italy is the *aceto balsamico* from Modena. Balsamic vinegar is a deep, reddish brown wine vinegar, flavored with herbs and aged in wood. It lends its distinctive sweet and sour flavor to any dish and so should be used with care. I do not recommend it for every salad (or every dish) and sometimes prefer a red or white wine vinegar.

Herbs

Fresh herbs add immeasurably to a dish and figure throughout Italian cooking. Basil, oregano, rosemary, mint, tarragon, and of course, Italian broadleaf parsley are those herbs used most frequently in the recipes that follow. All can be found fresh fairly easily, especially during the summer months, or can be grown from seed or seedlings. (Virtually anyone can grow basil, in a garden or window box, providing they have a warm, sunny spot. Once started, there never seems to be enough of this delightful herb.) Occasionally, you may have to use dried herbs and I have indicated in the recipe where this can be done.

Kitchen Equipment

Very few of the recipes in this book require any special equipment beyond the range of good sharp knives, several heavy-based sauté pans and saucepans, spoons, graters, whisks, and measuring cups and spoons that are the indispensable working tools of any practiced cook. For cooking pasta, however, you will need an 8-quart stockpot (and a good metal colander, preferably one that can stand alone), and if you want to make pizzas you'll need an 16-inch pizza pan or baking sheet. Otherwise, the few recipes that do need special equipment are clearly indicated.

Pasta and Ice Cream Machines

Pasta machines, either manual or electric, are becoming more widely used. Manual models are less expensive but require the user to work with the dough first to assure the proper consistency, and rolling-out width and thickness. The dough must be fed into the machine while hand-cranking, a process which requires two hands and concentration but which becomes easier with practice.

Electric machines eliminate the necessity of working with the dough until it is extruded from the machine. The machines come with their own measures which, for the most part, succeed in taking the guesswork out of ingredient amounts. Electric machines enable you to make fresh round and tubular pastas that are impossible or too time-consuming to make by hand or manual machine. (Dusting the formed pasta with semolina or cornmeal as it comes out of the machine prevents sticking together.) Cleaning electric machines is not always easy, especially the little holes in the pasta plates. Some models come with a special brush or tool to assist with this chore.

Ice cream machines are also available in various models and prices, and it is important to gauge your needs before making a choice. If you eat sherbets and ice creams only infrequently, you can follow the ice tray method described on Page 204, or invest in one of the less expensive, small-capacity models. Hand-crank models work very well, but are somewhat messy with their use of ice and coarse salt. If your family adores fresh ices, you may want a larger machine which can freeze them in a minimum amount of time. Larger machines are also more reliable in their timing (which is especially handy for entertaining at a moment's notice). Some of the models do not have removable bowls, but these do not seem overly difficult to clean if the manufacturer's instructions are followed. (But this is really the key to the best use of all these machines: read and follow the directions carefully for optimal results.)

CHAPTER 2

ANTIPASTI

Marinated vegetables are a popular appetizer in Italy, generally accompanying a leisurely aperitif before dinner. Normally, more than one vegetable is served at once to add variety. I have included several dishes here which may be made in advance, to be served as part of a mixed antipasto. With these dishes success depends as much on using only the freshest vegetables available and the best ingredients, such as extra virgin olive oil, as a judicious combination of colors, flavors, and textures. For example, I find the flavor and texture of Roast Peppers, probably the best-known vegetable appetizer, enhanced by pairing them with Marinated Zucchini. Of course, the simplest antipasto is raw or freshly blanched vegetables served with a basic Olive Oil Dip (Pinzimonio), which can be varied to suit your taste—ideal during summer months when good fresh vegetables are in abundance.

Most of the dishes that follow can equally be served as part of a main course. Caponata, while delicious alone or with fresh Italian bread as an appetizer, is often served as a relish, especially with egg and rice dishes.

Olives are almost always part of antipasti in Italy. There they can be found in enormous variety, ranging from deep black wrinkled olives produced near Rome, reddish-brown olives from Sardinia, and fat green olives of almost every shade and size. None bear very much resemblance to the almost tasteless variety sold in cans and jars in supermarkets in this country. Generally you can find good olives here sold loose, packed in oil or brine. Sometimes they are sold flavored with garlic or chili pepper, but you can add your own seasonings by putting a clove or two of peeled garlic or sprinkling rosemary or dried chili pepper into the jar. Stored in a tightly-sealed container in a cool place, they will keep almost indefinitely.

15

OLIVE OIL DIP
Pinzimonio

½ cup extra virgin olive oil

1 tablespoon Balsamic or white wine vinegar, or
    lemon juice

¼ teaspoon salt

A pinch of freshly ground pepper

Mix together the oil, vinegar or lemon juice, salt, and pepper. Serve in a bowl surrounded by raw vegetables such as radishes, carrots, celery, fennel, and cherry tomatoes; or asparagus, broccoli, and artichokes blanched briefly in salted boiling water, then refreshed in cold water and drained.

Serves 6. Preparation time: 5 minutes

MUSHROOMS WITH LEMON AND OIL
Funghi al Limone e Olio

1 pound small, tightly closed mushrooms

¼ cup lemon juice

½ cup olive oil, preferably extra virgin

1 garlic clove, minced

½ teaspoon salt

⅛ teaspoon freshly ground pepper

2 tablespoons finely chopped broadleaf parsley

Wipe the mushrooms with a damp cloth, and slice off the stems. Toss the mushrooms with the lemon juice in a saucepan. Add the olive oil, garlic, salt, pepper, and enough water just to cover the mushrooms. Set over high heat and toss gently a few times, being careful not to bruise the mushrooms. As soon as the liquid boils, remove from the heat and allow the mushrooms to cool in the broth. Toss with the parsley. Transfer to a jar, cover, and refrigerate for at least 1 hour. Return to room temperature before serving.

Serves 6. Preparation time: 15 minutes

COLD VEGETABLE PLATTER
Piatto Freddo di Ortaggi

4 or 5 small eggplants, unpeeled, in 1-inch dice

2 or 3 small zucchini, well scrubbed but unpeeled, in
    1-inch dice

1 teaspoon salt

½ recipe Roast Peppers (Page 19), in 1-inch dice

½ cup olive oil

½ cup water

½ cup thinly sliced onion

1 garlic clove, minced

1 small bay leaf

A pinch of thyme

⅛ teaspoon freshly ground pepper

2 tablespoons minced broadleaf parsley

Lightly salt the eggplant and zucchini and allow them to drain for 30 minutes. Preheat the oven to 375°. Toss all the ingredients except the parsley in a baking dish, cover and bake for 1 hour, stirring once. Turn out into another dish and allow to cool. Toss with the parsley. Cover and refrigerate for at least 1 hour before serving.

Serves 6. Preparation time: 1½ hours

FENNEL IN OLIVE OIL
Finocchio all'Olio

6 small fennel bulbs, or 3 large ones
¼ cup olive oil, preferably extra virgin
1 teaspoon salt
⅛ teaspoon freshly ground pepper
1 tablespoon white wine vinegar

Remove the outer layer and stalks from the fennel bulbs. Halve the bulbs and slice them thinly. Toss with the remaining ingredients. Serve immediately or cover and refrigerate. Serve at room temperature.
Serves 6. Preparation time: 5 minutes

MARINATED ZUCCHINI
Zucchini Marinati

6 small zucchini, 6 to 7-inches long
2 teaspoons salt
½ cup olive oil, preferably extra virgin
½ teaspoon freshly ground pepper
½ cup wine vinegar, preferably Balsamic
3 garlic cloves, minced
¼ cup fresh mint leaves

Wash the zucchini well and cut into slices about 3-inches by ½-inch. Toss with the salt and allow to drain on paper towels for 30 minutes. Heat ¼ cup of the oil in a skillet and sauté the zucchini over medium heat, turning frequently, for about 10 minutes, until just tender. Drain and season with pepper.

While the zucchini is cooking, heat the remaining ¼ cup oil, vinegar, and garlic in a small saucepan. When the mixture sizzles, remove from the heat. Toss the cooked zucchini with the hot vinegar and the mint leaves. Marinate for at least 2 hours, tossing occasionally. The zucchini may be refrigerated but should be served at room temperature.
Serves 6. Preparation time (not including marinating): 45 minutes

MARINATED CARROTS
Carote Marinate

24 baby carrots (about 1½ pounds)
2 scallions, sliced (green and white parts)
1½ tablespoons finely chopped broadleaf parsley
1 teaspoon finely chopped fresh oregano, or
    ¼ teaspoon dried
½ teaspoon salt
⅛ teaspoon freshly ground pepper
4 teaspoons red wine vinegar
3 tablespoons olive oil, preferably extra virgin
Broadleaf parsley for garnish

Peel the carrots and cook in lightly salted boiling water to cover for 8 minutes, or until tender but still firm when pierced with a knife. Drain and transfer to a shallow serving dish. Sprinkle the scallions, parsley, and oregano over carrots; season with salt and pepper. Toss lightly with the vinegar and oil. Allow to marinate for at least 3 to 4 hours at room temperature, tossing from time to time. (Refrigerate to marinate for a longer period, and return to room temperature before serving.) Serve the carrots in the marinade, garnished with parsley sprigs.
Serves 6. Preparation time (not including marinating): 15 minutes

 # ROAST PEPPERS
Peperoni Arrosto

The flavor obtained by charring the skins of sweet peppers is worth the effort, but it has never been one of my favorite tasks. The method for peeling peppers described below is the most efficient one I have found. Roast peppers are perfect for garnish, as an addition to almost any dish, from pizzas to frittatas, or as a salad by themselves.

8 green, red, or yellow bell peppers
¼ cup lemon juice
½ cup olive oil, preferably extra virgin
½ teaspoon salt
⅛ teaspoon freshly ground pepper

Preheat the broiler. Halve the peppers and remove their stems, seeds, and any white pith in their cavities. Flatten them with your hands as much as possible (this allows all surfaces to be exposed to the heat uniformly). Place the peppers on a roasting pan 3 inches from the heat and roast until their skin becomes black, turning them to ensure even charring. Remove the peppers from the pan and immediately put them into a paper bag just large enough to hold them. Close the bag tightly and allow the peppers to steam for 5 minutes, shaking the bag a few times to redistribute them. Remove the peppers and plunge them into cold water. Peel away the skin using a small knife and rinse the flesh with cool running water. Slice into ½-inch strips and toss with the remaining ingredients. Serve immediately or cover and refrigerate, then return to room temperature before serving.
Serves 6. Preparation time: 20 minutes

 # CAPONATA

As with many eggplant dishes, caponata originated in Catania in Sicily, where the Greek influence in cooking is almost as strong as the Italian. The popularity of caponata as a dip or relish is due to its mixture of sweet and sour; if you prefer a less pungent dish, substitute red wine for the vinegar.

4 or 5 small eggplants
¾ teaspoon salt
¼ cup olive oil
1½ cups finely chopped celery
1½ cups thinly sliced red onion
½ cup red wine vinegar, mixed with
    1½ teaspoons honey
1 pound plum tomatoes, chopped
1 teaspoon tomato paste
2 tablespoons capers
2 tablespoons raisins
3 ounces black olives in brine, pitted and
    coarsely chopped
½ teaspoon salt
⅛ teaspoon freshly ground pepper
1 tablespoon finely chopped broadleaf parsley

Cut the ends off the eggplants and dice them, unpeeled, into 1-inch cubes. Sprinkle with ¾ teaspoon salt and lay on a bed of paper towels. Put a plate or cutting board on top of the eggplant to help press out the bitter juices, and let stand for 30 minutes.

Heat 2 tablespoons of olive oil in a large skillet and sauté the celery over moderate heat, stirring frequently, for 5 minutes. Add the onion and continue to sauté for 8 to 10 minutes more, or until the vegetables are soft and lightly colored. Using a slotted spoon, transfer the vegetables to a bowl.

Rinse the eggplant with cold water and drain on paper towels. Heat the remaining 2 tablespoons olive oil in the skillet and sauté the eggplant, turning frequently, over medium heat for 8 to 10 minutes or until lightly browned in all sides. Return the celery and onion to the pan and stir in the vinegar and honey, tomatoes, tomato paste, capers, raisins, and olives. Season with salt and pepper. Bring to a boil and simmer uncovered for 15 minutes, stirring frequently. Add water if the mixture becomes dry and begins to stick. Taste and adjust seasonings, adding more salt, pepper, or vinegar accordingly. Transfer to a serving bowl and refrigerate. Serve cold, sprinkled with fresh parsley.
Serves 6. Preparation time: 1 hour

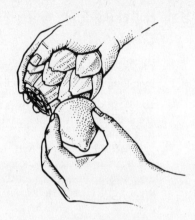

1 On a flat surface, trim off the artichoke stem and the tips of the leaves 1–inch from the ends.

2 Rub the cut parts of the artichoke with lemon to prevent discoloration.

3 Holding the artichoke by its base, press downwards in a circular motion to spread the leaves.

4 Press the filling firmly in the spaces between the leaves.

STUFFED ARTICHOKES
Carciofini Ripieni

Choose unblemished artichokes that are green and firm; each should have an inch-long stem to ensure its freshness.

3 cups fresh breadcrumbs
¾ cup freshly grated parmesan or romano
¼ cup finely chopped broadleaf parsley
2 teaspoons minced fresh oregano, or ¾ teaspoon dried
4 to 5 garlic cloves, minced
1 teaspoon salt
¼ teaspoon freshly ground pepper
½ cup olive oil
6 medium to large artichokes
2 lemons, quartered
¾ cup water
6 tablespoons olive oil

Combine the breadcrumbs, cheese, herbs, and garlic and season with salt and pepper. Add the olive oil, working it into the crumbs by rubbing it between the palms of your hands to distribute the oil evenly. Trim the stems of the artichokes and cut 1-inch from the top leaves. Rub any cut parts with lemon to prevent discoloration. Turn each artichoke upside down and in a circular motion press it against a hard surface to spread the leaves for stuffing. Holding the artichoke over the bowl of filling, take a small handful of the mixture and press it between the leaves. Stand the artichokes in a pan just large enough to hold them. Add the water and 6 tablespoons of olive oil. Bring to a boil, then cover, reduce the heat, and simmer for 30 to 45 minutes, depending on the size of the artichokes. The outer leaves will separate easily when they are done. Check the pan from time to time and add water as necessary.

Serve the artichokes immediately. A fork inserted in the center top of the artichoke will enable you to hold it stable while peeling off the outer layers. The stuffing will come away with the leaves. When the leaves are almost gone, remove the fibrous choke to expose the tender artichoke bottom.
Serves 6. Preparation time: 1¼ hours

TOMATOES STUFFED WITH VEGETABLES
Pomodori con Ripieno di Verdura

Though the cooking times do not differ substantially, I prefer to cook the vegetables separately for this recipe. This makes it easier to test for that slightly crunchy stage that captures the flavor and freshness of each vegetable. Start with potatoes because of their neutral color and flavor and end with green beans, which have the most dominant flavor. In a pinch you may cook them all together, though I don't recommend it.

6 large ripe tomatoes
Salt to taste
Freshly ground pepper to taste
1 cup Garlic Mayonnaise (Page 50)
1½ cups new or red potatoes, in ½-inch dice
1½ cups carrots, in ½-inch dice
1 cup shelled fresh peas or frozen peas
1½ cups green beans, in ½-inch dice
Fresh basil

Slice ½-inch from the top of each tomato and scoop out the seeds, leaving a shell at least ½-inch thick. Salt and pepper the insides of the tomatoes, if desired. Make the garlic mayonnaise.

Cook the potatoes in salted boiling water until just tender, about 5 minutes. Lift out with a slotted spoon and immediately refresh in cold water. When cool, drain. Continue with the carrots, peas, and beans, cooking each until tender but still crunchy. Spread on paper towels to dry. In a mixing bowl, toss the vegetables with the mayonnaise, starting with ½ cup and adding more until they are lightly coated. (The colors should not be overwhelmed by the mayonnaise, nor should the mixture be soupy. You may pass extra mayonnaise separately.) Fill each tomato with the vegetable mixture, mounding it at the top and garnishing with a basil leaf. Serve immediately or refrigerate.

Serves 6. Preparation time: 45 minutes

EGGPLANT STUFFED WITH TOMATOES AND OLIVES
Melanzane Ripiene con Pomodori e Olive

This hearty dish can be served as an appetizer, a side dish, and even a main course. Use small eggplants for a side dish to accompany an entrée. Appetizer portions call for a slightly larger vegetable to allow half an eggplant per person (avoid the largest ones, which tend to be bitter).

6 small eggplants

1 teaspoon salt

½ cup olive oil

4 plum tomatoes, peeled, seeded, and chopped

½ cup pitted black olives

1 tablespoon small capers, rinsed and drained

¼ teaspoon freshly ground pepper

3 tablespoons finely chopped broadleaf parsley

½ cup fresh breadcrumbs

3 tablespoons freshly grated parmesan

Cut the eggplants in half lengthwise, sprinkle with salt and let them drain on paper towels for 15 minutes. Meanwhile, bring a large pot of water to boil. Scoop out the eggplant pulp and reserve. Drop the shells into the boiling water, boil for 5 minutes, then refresh immediately with cold water. Preheat the oven to 375°.

Heat ¼ cup olive oil in a large skillet. Chop the eggplant pulp and sauté it for 10 minutes, until lightly browned. Add the tomatoes, olives, capers, and pepper and continue to cook until the tomato juices have evaporated, about 10 minutes. Remove from heat and toss with ¼ cup breadcrumbs and parsley. Lightly salt and pepper the cavities of the eggplant shells and fill them with this mixture. Place them on a baking sheet. Mix the remaining ¼ cup breadcrumbs with the cheese and sprinkle on top of the filling. Drizzle the remaining olive oil over the breadcrumbs and bake for 20 minutes. Serve immediately.

Serves 6. Preparation time: 1 hour

DEEP-FRIED VEGETABLES
Fritto Misto

For a classic garnish, deep-fry sprigs of broadleaf parsley without batter for a crisp, green accompaniment.

2 or 3 small zucchini, well-scrubbed but unpeeled,
   in 2-inch by ¼-inch sticks
½ pound carrots, peeled, in 2-inch by ¼-inch sticks
12 thin asparagus spears, cut in 2-inch lengths
1 bunch scallions, cut in 2-inch lengths
½ pound fresh mushrooms
3 cups water
2 cups flour
1 to 2 cups vegetable oil for deep-frying
Salt to taste
Freshly ground pepper to taste
Lemon wedges
Broadleaf parsley

Prepare the vegetables. Parboil the carrots in salted water for 2 minutes, rinse with cold water, and drain. Wipe the mushrooms with a damp cloth and trim stems. Preheat oven to 300°.

Put the water in a bowl and mix in the flour by sifting small amounts onto the surface of the water and whisking it in. The batter should be thick, creamy, and have the smooth consistency of sour cream.

Heat the oil to 360° (see Page 12). Dip the vegetables into the batter, then slip them carefully into the hot oil. Fry in batches, being careful not to overcrowd, until golden brown on one side; then turn them and fry the other side. Remove with a slotted spoon and drain on paper towels; transfer to a serving platter, and keep warm in the oven until all the vegetables are fried. Regulate the heat of the oil to keep it at 360°, pausing between batches to allow it to reheat. When all the vegetables are cooked, season with salt and pepper, garnish the platter with lemon wedges and deep-fried parsley, and serve immediately.
Serves 6. Preparation time: 45 minutes

DEEP-FRIED MOZZARELLA
Mozzarella Milanese

Variations of deep-fried cheeses are found all over Italy. Mozzarella is used in this version; it can be made with bel paese, Italian fontina, or any semi-soft cheese that has a melting capability. To give the cheese a nutty flavor, add a tablespoon or two of sesame seeds to the breadcrumbs.

1 pound mozzarella
½ cup flour
4 eggs
2 tablespoons olive oil
½ teaspoon salt
⅛ teaspoon freshly ground pepper
6 cups fresh breadcrumbs
1 to 2 cups vegetable oil for deep-frying
1 cup Fresh Herb Sauce (Page 55)
1 cup Summer or Winter Tomato Sauce (Page 46)
Broadleaf parsley or fresh basil for garnish

Cut the mozzarella into pieces 4-inches long and ½-inch thick. Flour the cheese sticks, patting the flour well into each surface. Mix together the eggs, the olive oil, salt, and pepper. Dip the mozzarella in the egg mixture, then roll in breadcrumbs, patting the crumbs into each side. Dip the sticks again in the egg mixture. Roll them in the breadcrumbs a second time, pressing gently but firmly to make sure that the crumbs adhere to all sides and to the ends. (This careful coating will prevent the cheese from leaking through as it melts.) Refrigerate the breaded cheese for at least 30 minutes. Make or reheat the sauces.

Preheat the oven to 400°. In a deep-fryer or large, deep pot, heat the oil to 360° (see Page 12). Fry the cheese in batches until golden brown, turning once. Remove with a slotted spoon and drain on paper towels; allow the oil to reheat between batches. Serve the fried cheese immediately or keep warm on a baking sheet in the oven.

To serve, spoon the two sauces on opposite sides of heated dessert plates; top with the cheese. Serve at once, garnished with fresh parsley or basil.
Serves 6 (about 24 sticks). Preparation time (not including making sauces): 1 hour

SPINACH CROQUETTES
Polpettine di Spinaci

These spinach croquettes may be made in advance up to the point of deep-frying and refrigerated until you are ready to fry. (For advice on deep-frying, see Page 12.)

2 pounds fresh spinach, thoroughly washed

4 slices Italian bread, crusts removed

½ cup milk

2 tablespoons butter, at room temperature

1 teaspoon salt

⅛ teaspoon freshly ground pepper

2 tablespoons fresh breadcrumbs

2 tablespoons freshly grated parmesan

2 eggs

2 egg yolks

2 garlic cloves, minced

2 tablespoons currants

2 tablespoons chopped pine nuts

¼ teaspoon nutmeg

1 to 2 cups vegetable oil for deep frying

Steam the spinach in the water clinging to its leaves by placing it in a covered saucepan over medium-high heat for 5 minutes or until the leaves are just wilted. Drain and cool. Remove excess liquid by hand or by squeezing the spinach between two dinner plates and coarsely chop. Soak the bread slices in milk for 10 minutes; squeeze dry.

In a bowl, combine the spinach and all the other ingredients except the oil and mix well. Form teaspoonfuls of the mixture into balls. Heat about 2 inches of oil to 360°. Deep-fry the croquettes in batches until golden, about 1 minute, letting the oil return to 360° after each batch. Keep warm in a 300° oven until ready to serve.
Serves 6. Preparation time: 30 minutes

OLIVE AND CHEESE CANAPÉS
Pizzette con Olive

These canapés are made with gorgonzola crackers and mascarpone. Mascarpone, a cheese made from the rich cream of the Lombardy region, may be found in specialty cheese shops. Cream cheese can be substituted, but it lacks the freshness and texture of mascarpone.

1 pound mascarpone, or cream cheese
12 black olives, pitted
12 green olives, pitted
1 recipe Gorgonzola Crackers (Page 169)

Beat the cheese with a wooden spoon until smooth. Slice the olives into rounds or strips. Spread 1 teaspoon of cheese on each cracker and arrange the olive pieces on top.
Serves 6. Preparation time (not including crackers): 15 minutes

 # POLENTA CANAPÉS
Crostini di Polenta

This interesting use of polenta is typical of the region around Rome. Though the canapés may also be baked on a buttered baking sheet in a 375° oven for 20 minutes, I prefer the crisp texture achieved by deep-frying them (see Page 12). Deep-fried and cooled, the canapés may be frozen in sealed plastic bags for later use; simply crisp them in a 400° oven for 15 minutes before adding your preferred garnish.

½ recipe Polenta (Page 116)
1 to 2 cups vegetable oil for deep-frying
⅔ cup mascarpone
½ cup shelled and coarsely chopped pistachios
1 cup Sweet and Sour Tomato Sauce (Page 47)
1 cup freshly grated mozzarella
2 tablespoons small capers, rinsed and drained

Prepare the polenta and spread to a ¼-inch thickness. When cool, cut it into diamond-shaped pieces by making parallel cuts 1-inch apart top to bottom, then diagonal cuts left top to right bottom. Heat the oil to 350°–370° in a deep-fryer or similar pot. Fry the polenta in batches of 6 to 12, depending on the size of the pot. Cook 3 to 5 minutes, until golden brown, turning once with a slotted spoon. Drain on paper towels.

Preheat the broiler. Beat the mascarpone until smooth and spread on half the canapés. Sprinkle with the chopped pistachios and pat the nuts into the cheese. Place on a serving platter, leaving room for the other canapés. Heat the tomato sauce and spread a little on each remaining canapé. Sprinkle with the mozzarella and garnish with the capers. Just before serving, broil until the cheese melts, about 1 minute. Arrange on the serving platter with the pistachio canapés and serve immediately.

Serves 6. Preparation time (not including making polenta): 40 minutes

CHAPTER 3

SOUPS

S tocks are produced to derive the essences of flavor, be it from vegetables, meat, or fish, for use in soups and sauces and risottos. Simmering sautéed, roasted, or boiled vegetables breaks down their fibers to release all their flavor into the liquid. This requires slow cooking, but once the vegetables are put on to simmer, the stock has no need of constant attention. You can make up a large quantity of stock from whatever vegetables are on hand added to the basic aromatics— onions, carrots, and celery. It will keep for several weeks in the refrigerator and needs only reboiling once a week to keep it fresh. For most of my recipes it is probably easier to keep the stock frozen in 4 to 6 cup quantities. You can make a vegetable glaze by boiling down the stock to a thick, syrupy essence. The glaze can also be frozen in ice cube trays and reconstituted with water as needed.

The two stocks described below offer a range which can fill any culinary voids left by meat. The brown stock is rich in color and flavor, for hearty soups and sauces. The white stock allows us to enjoy risotto, the Milanese favorite. In the white stock, the vegetables are simply boiled together without the use of fats or oils, making it unnecessary to clarify the stock for use in clear soups.

After the stocks is a recipe for clarification, which applies especially to the brown stock to prepare it for use as a consommé.

Homemade vegetable stocks are vastly preferable to prepared products. However, instant vegetable broth cubes or powders can be substituted if necessary. Be careful to taste the soup or sauce carefully before adding any salt though as instant cubes or powders have generally been well-seasoned by the manufacturer.

WHITE STOCK

3 large onions, cubed
3 or 4 carrots, cubed
1 large leek, white part only, cubed
2 stalks celery, cubed
1 head garlic, separated but unpeeled
1½ cups mushrooms, quartered and sprinkled with
    lemon juice
Bouquet garni:
    Tie together in cheesecloth 1 bunch of
    parsley, stems only; 1 large bay leaf; 2 teaspoons
    fresh leaf thyme or ½ teaspoon dried; 1 teaspoon
    white peppercorns
2 cups dry white wine
4 quarts water

Place all the ingredients in a stockpot and bring to a boil. Simmer over low heat for 4 to 5 hours to allow the vegetables to render all their juices. Add hot water if necessary. Remove the bouquet garni and pass the liquid through a fine sieve. Discard the vegetables.

    The stock may be refrigerated or frozen. If kept in the refrigerator, it should be reheated once a week to keep it fresh-tasting.
Yield: 2 quarts. Preparation time: 5 hours

 # BROWN STOCK

3 large onions, cubed
3 or 4 carrots, cubed
2 stalks celery, cubed
1 large leek, white and tender green parts, cubed
2 cups parsnips, cubed
12 radishes, halved
¼ cup olive oil
¼ cup vegetable oil
2 cups dry white wine

2 cups mushrooms, quartered and sprinkled with
   lemon juice
2 tablespoons vegetable oil
4 quarts water
1 tablespoon tomato paste
Bouquet garni:
   Tie together in cheesecloth 1 bunch parsley;
   1 large bay leaf; 2 teaspoons fresh leaf thyme, or
   ½ teaspoon dried; 1 teaspoon black peppercorns

Preheat the oven to 450°. Combine all the vegetables except the mushrooms in a roasting pan; toss with the oils. (The vegetable oil allows the olive oil to come to a higher temperature without burning.) Roast until well browned, about 1 hour, stirring once. Transfer to a stock pot.

Pour the wine into the roasting pan and bring to a boil on the stove top, scraping up all the brown residue from the vegetables. Add this liquid to the stockpot. In a separate pan, sauté the mushrooms in 2 tablespoons of oil over high heat until well browned. Add them to the stockpot, along with the water, tomato paste, and bouquet garni. Bring the stock to a boil and simmer for 8 hours, adding hot water as necessary. Strain through a fine sieve and discard the vegetables. The stock may be refrigerated or frozen. Skim the fat layer from the top of the stock before using.
Yield: 2 quarts. Preparation time: 9 hours

 # CLARIFICATION OF VEGETABLE STOCK

½ cup chopped onion
¼ cup chopped carrot
¼ cup chopped celery
½ cup chopped leek
2 tablespoons finely chopped
   fresh herbs, suitable to recipe
1 egg white
1 egg shell, crumbled
5 cups vegetable stock

In a bowl, mix together the vegetables and herbs, egg white and shell. Skim the stock of any fat and mix 1 cup with the vegetables. Pour the remaining stock into a large saucepan and whisk in the vegetable mixture. Slowly bring to a simmer, stirring frequently. Once the liquid has come to a simmer, stop stirring. The mixture will be cloudy and a 'clarifying crust' will form. Pull the pan to the side of the heat so that the liquid simmers up through the crust in one spot only. Regulate the heat so that the liquid simmers gently and never boils. Every 15 minutes turn the pot a quarter turn to form a new clarification 'hole'. Line a fine sieve with a double thickness of wet cheesecloth or a paper coffee filter. After 1 hour, skim the clarification crust gently into the sieve and strain the stock. Discard the vegetable mixture.
Yield: 1 quart. Preparation time: 1¼ hours

 # SPICY COLD TOMATO SOUP
Zuppa Fredda al Pomodoro

This soup, which originated in the Mediterranean town of Genoa, is a lighter version of its sister soup from Spain, *gazpacho*.

12 slices stale Italian bread

1 pound ripe tomatoes, preferably plum

1 cup chopped onion

1 cucumber

1 tablespoon finely chopped fresh basil

A 1-inch piece of hot chili pepper, minced, or
    4 drops Tabasco

5 tablespoons olive oil, preferably extra virgin

2 tablespoons red wine vinegar

1 cup cold water

1½ teaspoons salt

¼ teaspoon freshly ground pepper

¼ cup coarsely chopped fresh basil

Soak the bread in cold water for 10 minutes. Squeeze it dry, place in a mixing bowl, and reserve. To peel the tomatoes, score their bottoms and blanch for 30 seconds in boiling water. Refresh immediately in cold water and peel. Core the tomatoes, halve and seed them, then

chop coarsely, reserving the juices. Add the tomatoes, their juice, and onion to the bread. Peel the cucumber and halve lengthwise. Scoop out the seeds with a spoon and discard. Chop the cucumber and add with all the other ingredients, except the ¼ cup basil, to the tomatoes. Purée the mixture in a blender, food processor, or food mill. Chill the soup until ready to serve. Garnish with basil before serving.
Serves 6. Preparation time: 20 minutes

 ## SPINACH SOUP
Minestra di Spinaci

2 pounds fresh spinach, or 2 10-ounce packages
    frozen spinach
¼ cup butter
2 cups milk
2 cups water
1½ teaspoons salt
¼ teaspoon freshly ground pepper
⅛ teaspoon grated nutmeg
¼ cup heavy cream
2 tablespoons finely chopped fresh basil or
    broadleaf parsley
5 tablespoons freshly grated parmesan

Remove the stems from the spinach and wash the leaves thoroughly in several changes of cold water. Cook the spinach in the water clinging to its leaves in a covered saucepan over medium-high heat just until wilted. Drain immediately and allow to cool. (If using frozen spinach, allow to thaw.) Squeeze out the excess moisture by hand or by pressing the spinach between two plates. Chop the spinach. Heat the butter in a saucepan and sauté the spinach briefly. Add the milk, water, salt, pepper, and nutmeg, and bring to a boil. Immediately lower the heat and simmer 5 minutes. Stir in the cream, fresh basil or parsley, and cheese and serve at once.

To serve the soup chilled, refrigerate after the simmer and add the cream and fresh basil or parsley just before serving, omitting the grated cheese.
Serves 6. Preparation time: 30 minutes

RAVIOLINI IN BROTH
Raviolini in Brodo

Homemade pasta in broth is a wonderful treat. In this recipe, fresh raviolini are used, but any small pasta may be substituted. For a lovely clear broth, the raviolini are precooked and rinsed so that none of their surface starch remains. If the pasta were cooked in the broth, this starch would muddy its clarity.

2 quarts clarified Brown Stock (Page 32)
½ recipe Ravioli (Page 78), shaped in ¾-inch squares
Salt and freshly ground pepper to taste
2 tablespoons chopped fresh basil or broadleaf parsley
¼ cup freshly grated parmesan

Make the stock and clarify it according to the directions on Page 33; set aside. Prepare the raviolini and allow them to dry. In a large pot, bring 4 quarts of water to a boil and add salt. Gently drop in the raviolini and cook, stirring frequently, until they reach the *al dente* stage, about 6 to 8 minutes. Drain immediately and refresh in cold water, separating them so that they do not stick together.

Five minutes before serving, bring the stock to a boil and season with salt and pepper. Drain the raviolini and carefully stir into the hot stock. Simmer just until the raviolini are reheated. Ladle into a warmed soup tureen or individual bowls and sprinkle with basil or parsley. Serve immediately, passing the grated cheese separately.
Serves 6. Preparation time (not including stock): 1 hour

 # ONION AND CHEESE SOUP
Zuppa di Cipolle e Fontina

When I found that the Brown Stock had as robust a flavor and color as any meat stock I had tasted, I couldn't resist the temptation to make an onion soup with it. Grappa is an Italian brandy particularly well loved by the Alpine mountaineers of the north who are often served this warming combination of hearty soup and spirits.

6 tablespoons butter
6 cups thinly sliced onion
2 quarts Brown Stock (Page 32)

1½ teaspoons salt

½ teaspoon freshly ground pepper

5 tablespoons grappa or brandy

12 slices Italian bread, toasted

1 pound coarsely grated Italian fontina

Heat the butter in a large saucepan and sauté the onions gently until golden and translucent, about 10 minutes. Pour in the stock, bring to a boil, and season with salt and pepper. Cover and simmer for 30 minutes. Stir in the brandy.

Preheat the broiler. Place half the toasts in the bottom of a heatproof soup tureen or individual crocks. Sprinkle with ⅓ of the grated cheese. Ladle the soup into the bowl(s), then top with the remaining toasts and cheese. Place the bowl(s) 5 inches from the broiler for 1 or 2 minutes, just until the cheese is melted and slightly browned. Serve immediately.

Serves 6. Preparation time (not including stock): 1 hour

 # ARUGULA VICHYSSOISE
Zuppa Freddo di Ruchetta

Arugula's young leaves are tastiest when picked before they grow to more than 4 inches, and the brief cooking time in this soup allows the leaves to retain their bright green color and fresh flavor. This vichyssoise can be served hot or chilled; it will keep in the refrigerator for several days.

½ cup chopped leeks, white and tender green parts

1 cup chopped onion

2 pounds potatoes, in 1-inch dice

6 cups water

2 teaspoons salt

¼ teaspoon freshly ground pepper

4 cups arugula leaves, thoroughly washed

½ cup heavy cream

Combine the leeks, onion, and potatoes with water in a large saucepan. Season with salt and pepper and bring to a boil. Simmer for 20 to 30 minutes, until the potatoes are tender. Stir in the arugula and as soon as the leaves have wilted, about 30 seconds, remove the pan from the

heat. Purée the soup in a blender, food processor, or food mill and return to the pan. Bring back to a boil, then simmer the soup while stirring in the cream. Serve hot, or pour into a heat-proof container and refrigerate for at least 2 hours before serving chilled.
Serves 6. Preparation time: 45 minutes

 # ZUCCHINI SOUP
Zuppa di Zucchini

¼ cup butter

½ cup chopped onion

3 or 4 medium zucchini (about 1½ pounds), well
    scrubbed but unpeeled, in ½-inch dice

8 cups White Stock (Page 32)

2 teaspoons salt

¼ teaspoon freshly ground pepper

2 eggs

¼ cup freshly grated parmesan

1 tablespoon minced fresh oregano, or 1 teaspoon dried

2 tablespoons minced fresh basil

Heat the butter in a large saucepan and sauté the onion gently until golden and translucent, about 5 minutes. Add the zucchini and sauté 10 minutes over medium-low heat. Stir in the stock and bring to a boil; season with salt and pepper. Cover and simmer 10 minutes, until the zucchini is quite tender. Purée the soup in a blender, food processor, or food mill and return it to the saucepan. Reheat the soup to a simmer. Whisk together the eggs, cheese, and herbs; pour them into the soup and whisk gently just until the eggs have set, about 30 seconds. Serve immediately.
Serves 6. Preparation time (not including stock): 30 minutes

MINESTRONI

Minestrones are a favorite of the Italian cook because they can be adapted to every season and budget. Traditionally, they included whatever could be found at the market that was fresh, appealing, and moderately priced—in short, whatever was in season. Each region had its own crops, which are reflected in the makeup of their minestrones, and I have included two as representative of this diversity.

Minestrone Milanese is a northern soup, with subtle spicing and the rice that is a staple in the region. In contrast, the soup from Calabria is a fiery rendition of vegetable stew, with a base of tomatoes and chili pepper and the addition of dry macaroni.

MINESTRONE ALLA MILANESE

This soup is enhanced by the addition of a *battuto*, a paste made with aromatic vegetables and herbs chopped until they disintegrate so that they release their flavors directly into a soup or stew and also serve as a thickening agent. A *battuto* includes the neutral vegetables celery, carrot, and onion, to which a distinctive herb is added—in this case, basil. Sage, thyme, oregano, fennel, and other herbs can be used equally well.

Battuto:
¼ cup chopped celery
½ cup chopped onion
¼ cup chopped carrot
1 tablespoon minced fresh basil
3 tablespoons olive oil

Soup:
2 quarts water
3 teaspoons salt
½ teaspoon freshly ground pepper
¼ cup dried chickpeas, soaked overnight, or ½ cup
  canned chickpeas, drained
2 plum tomatoes, peeled, seeded, and chopped
2 potatoes, in ½-inch dice
1 cup cauliflower, in small florets
¼ cup chopped celery

½ cup chopped carrots

½ cup rice, preferably Arborio

¼ cup chopped onion

1 cup shredded cabbage

2 cups escarole, thoroughly washed, in 1-inch dice

2 cups Italian curly endive, thoroughly washed, in
    1-inch dice

1 cup fresh spinach, thoroughly washed

½ cup shelled fresh peas or frozen peas

2 tablespoons minced broadleaf parsley

To prepare the *battuto*, finely chop the celery, onion, and carrot with the basil until their juices are rendered and the mixture resembles a paste. Heat the olive oil in a large saucepan and sauté the *battuto* gently until it is golden and fragrant, about 10 minutes. Regulate the heat so that the mixture does not brown. Add the water to the pot and bring to a boil; season with salt and pepper. Stir in the chickpeas and tomatoes and simmer for 1 hour or until the chickpeas are tender. Add the potatoes, cauliflower, celery, carrots, rice, and onion, and continue to simmer for 10 minutes. Add the remaining ingredients and simmer until the peas are just tender, about 8 to 10 minutes. Serve hot, with toasted Italian bread and freshly grated parmesan.

Serves 6 as a main course. Preparation time: 1¾ hours

 ## MINESTRONE ALLA CALABRESE

¼ cup olive oil

¼ cup vegetable oil

1 cup chopped onion

1 garlic clove, minced

2 tablespoons finely chopped hot chili pepper

6 cups water, approximately

4 fresh basil leaves

2 teaspoons salt

½ teaspoon freshly ground pepper

2 pounds tomatoes, with their juice; peeled, seeded, and
    coarsely chopped, or 2 32-ounce cans Italian plum
    tomatoes, drained, seeded, and coarsely chopped

1 tablespoon tomato paste

1 cup red kidney beans, soaked overnight

½ cup chopped red pepper

½ cup chopped green pepper

1 cup small shell macaroni

2 tablespoons minced fresh basil

¼ teaspoon cracked red pepper flakes, or to taste

Heat the oils in a large saucepan and sauté the onion gently until golden and translucent, about 5 minutes. Add the garlic and chili pepper and sauté 3 minutes more. Add the water and bring to a boil. Season with salt and pepper and basil. Stir in the tomatoes, paste, and beans, simmer for 1½ hours, until the beans are just tender. Add the red and green peppers and simmer 5 minutes. Bring the soup to a boil and add the macaroni. Boil 5 to 10 minutes, stirring frequently, until the macaroni is just *al dente*. Stir in the fresh basil and pepper flakes. Serve hot, with freshly grated parmesan and toasted Italian bread.
Serves 6 as a main course. Preparation time: 2¼ hours

 # ESCAROLE AND RICE SOUP
Zuppa di Scarola e Riso

If you are unable to find escarole in your market, romaine lettuce is a milder flavored substitute.

2 heads escarole

¼ cup butter

½ cup chopped onion

4 cups water

2 teaspoons salt

½ teaspoon freshly ground pepper

¼ cup rice, preferably Arborio

2 tablespoons minced fresh basil or broadleaf parsley,
    or a combination of the two

3 tablespoons freshly grated parmesan

Trim the escarole of any bruised leaves and wash thoroughly in cold water. Cut into ½-inch strips. Heat the butter in a large saucepan and

sauté the onion until golden and translucent. Add the escarole and sauté briefly, just to coat with butter. Add the water, bring to a boil, and season with salt and pepper. Cover and simmer for 30 minutes, until the greens are tender. Stir in the rice, cover, and simmer gently for 15 minutes, until the rice is cooked but still firm. Remove from the heat, stir in the herbs and cheese, and serve.
Serves 6. Preparation time: 1 hour

 # TUSCAN BEAN SOUP
Zuppa di Fagioli Toscana

This hearty soup makes a nourishing and filling main course. The parmesan rind adds some of the saltiness of the more traditional rasher of bacon.

2 cups dried cannellini or great northern beans,
  soaked overnight
3 tablespoons olive oil
2 garlic cloves, minced
½ cup finely chopped onion
¼ cup finely chopped carrot
¼ cup finely chopped celery
½ cup finely chopped leek
2 teaspoons minced fresh rosemary, or
  ½ teaspoon dried
A 1-inch piece hot chili pepper, or to taste
A 4-inch piece of parmesan rind
2 teaspoons salt
½ teaspoon freshly ground pepper

Garnish:
½ cup extra virgin olive oil
1 garlic clove, minced
A pinch of thyme
6 to 8 slices toasted Italian bread
¾ cup freshly grated parmesan
12 thin slices red onion, separated into rings

Drain the beans. Heat the oil in a large saucepan and sauté the garlic, vegetables, rosemary, and pepper until lightly browned, about 10 minutes. Add the beans, parmesan rind, and water to cover. Season with salt and pepper, and simmer gently for 1 hour, until the beans are tender. Remove the parmesan rind and purée half the beans in the liquid. Return the purée to the saucepan and bring to a simmer, adding 3 to 4 cups water to make a thick soup.

To garnish, heat the extra virgin olive oil in a small skillet and sauté the garlic and thyme until golden. Stir half this oil mixture into the soup. Place the toasts in the bottom of a soup tureen or in individual crocks. Ladle in the soup and sprinkle it with the grated cheese, onion slices, and remaining oil. Serve immediately.

Serves 6. Preparation time: 1½ hours

 # ARTICHOKE AND FRESH PEA SOUP
Minestra di Carciofi e Piselli Freschi

This soup is good hot or chilled. To serve hot, garnish it with freshly grated pecorino or parmesan; for a chilled soup, refrigerate for 2 hours, stir in ⅓ cup heavy cream, and garnish with fresh mint leaves.

8 small artichokes, or 1 10-ounce package frozen
    artichoke hearts, thawed
¼ cup lemon juice dissolved in
    2 cups water (for fresh artichokes)
¼ cup olive oil
¼ cup chopped onion
1 garlic clove, minced
2 pounds fresh peas, shelled, or 2 10-ounce packages
    frozen peas
6 cups water
1½ teaspoons salt
¼ teaspoon freshly ground pepper
2 teaspoons minced fresh mint
1 tablespoon minced broadleaf parsley

Peel away the outer leaves of the artichokes with a small, sharp knife. Cut off the tips of the leaves and the artichoke stems. Halve the artichokes and core the choke with a melon baller. Quarter the hearts and immediately drop them into a bowl with the lemon juice and water.

Heat the oil in a large saucepan and sauté the onion and garlic until golden and translucent, about 8 to 10 minutes. Add ¾ of the peas and 6 cups water and bring to a boil. Season with salt, pepper, and mint. Simmer until the peas are tender, about 10 minutes.

Purée the soup in its liquid and pass through a sieve, making sure to press the pea pulp from the skins. Return the purée to the saucepan, bring to a boil and add the drained artichoke hearts. Boil for 15 minutes, stirring frequently to prevent the soup from sticking to the pan. When the artichokes are almost tender, add the remaining peas and simmer 8 to 10 minutes more. Stir in the parsley and serve hot or chilled, as above.

Serves 6. Preparation time: 1 hour

CHAPTER 4

SAUCES

A large book could be written on Italian sauces and still not cover the subject adequately. Unlike French sauces, there are no set rules for preparing them, and an Italian cook will produce a sauce that is as much a reflection of personal taste as it is of the particular regional cuisine. Accordingly, I have selected some of my favorites, at the same time attempting to present as broad a range of flavors and styles as possible.

Tomato sauces are almost universal and marry well with almost any pasta, egg, or cheese dish. The béchamel-based sauces are typical of the creamier style of northern cooking, whereas the classic Pesto has its origins in the northwest. The richer Wild Mushroom Sauce adds an exotic touch to a plain risotto or freshly made fettucine, while the Mushroom Marsala Sauce can be served equally as a dish by itself.

Many of the sauces that follow can be made ahead and kept frozen in tightly-sealed containers for future use. I find this particularly helpful when good fresh tomatoes are readily available during the summer months, or when I can find plenty of fresh herbs at the market and am able to preserve their flavors in a pesto for use on pasta or vegetable dishes or salads during the winter months.

In the following chapters, I have included some suggestions for serving these sauces. Naturally, there are dozens of other pastas, rice and grain dishes, salads, and vegetables that they can be served with; and you should by no means be limited by the few ideas I have been able to present here. Each of the recipes makes enough for about six servings but, of course, this depends on the type of pasta or dish you are serving.

SUMMER TOMATO SAUCE
Salsa di Pomodori Estiva

This extremely simple sauce is lighter than the winter sauce but it can be used in many of the same dishes. The vegetables and herbs of summer allow you to vary it at will, depending on what is fresh in your garden or at the market. Consider adding peppers, fresh oregano, or chilis ... and experiment to find the flavors you enjoy most.

6 tablespoons butter

3 pounds fresh tomatoes, preferably Italian plum;
   peeled, seeded, and chopped

¼ cup minced fresh basil

1 teaspoon salt

¼ teaspoon freshly ground pepper

Melt the butter in a large skillet. Stir in the remaining ingredients and simmer for 15 minutes.

    To store the sauce, cool to room temperature, cover and refrigerate for up to 2 weeks.

Makes 3 cups. Preparation time: 25 minutes

WINTER TOMATO SAUCE
Salsa d'Inverno

This is a savory sauce to make during the months when fresh tomatoes are not available. Vary it by adding ½ cup fresh fennel, a little citrus rind, or other dried herbs.

¼ cup olive oil

2 garlic cloves, minced

1 32-ounce can Italian plum tomatoes, coarsely
   chopped, and their juice

1 teaspoon tomato paste

1 teaspoon dried oregano

1 teaspoon salt

½ teaspoon freshly ground pepper

In a large skillet, heat the oil and sauté the garlic until it begins to turn golden. Add the tomatoes with their juices, the tomato paste, oregano, salt, and pepper. Cover and bring to a boil. Simmer for 10 minutes, then uncover and continue to simmer for a further 15 minutes. Serve immediately or cool to room temperature, cover, and refrigerate for up to 2 weeks. This sauce freezes very well.

Makes 3 cups. Preparation time: 30 minutes

 # SWEET AND SOUR TOMATO SAUCE
Salsa Agrodolce

2 pounds ripe tomatoes, preferably Italian plum, or 2
    32-ounce cans plum tomatoes, plus juice from cans

1 tablespoon olive oil

1½ cups chopped onion

2 tablespoons minced broadleaf parsley

2 tablespoons minced fresh basil

1 tablespoon tomato paste, if using fresh tomatoes

2 cups water, if using fresh tomatoes

1 tablespoon honey dissolved in 2 tablespoons
    red wine vinegar

½ teaspoon cinnamon

1 teaspoon salt

¼ teaspoon freshly ground pepper

Peel, seed, and chop the tomatoes; set aside. In a medium saucepan, heat the oil and sauté the onion and herbs gently for 5 minutes, until the onion begins to turn golden. Add all the other ingredients, stir, and cook over high heat, stirring occasionally, for 20 minutes, until the sauce is thick but the tomatoes still have some body. Serve hot or cool to room temperature, cover, and refrigerate.

Makes 3 cups. Preparation time: 45 minutes

COLD TOMATO SAUCE
Salsa Fredda di Pomodori

2 pounds ripe tomatoes, preferably Italian plum
½ cup olive oil
1 garlic clove, minced
A 2-inch piece hot chili pepper, seeded and minced,
    or ¼ teaspoon red pepper flakes, or to taste
1 teaspoon salt
¼ teaspoon freshly ground pepper
¼ cup minced fresh basil

To facilitate peeling, core the tomatoes and score their skins on the bottom with a small 'x'. Plunge them in batches into boiling water for 20 to 30 seconds. Refresh immediately in cold water. Peel and halve the tomatoes and scoop out their seeds. Chop them coarsely and toss with the remaining ingredients. Serve immediately or allow the tomatoes to marinate in the refrigerator for at least 1 hour, then serve at room temperature.
Makes 3 cups. Preparation time: 15 minutes

 # TOMATO VODKA SAUCE
Salsa di Pomodori e Vodka

1 pound plum tomatoes or 1 32-ounce can plum
    tomatoes, drained, peeled, seeded, and
    coarsely chopped
¾ cup vodka
A 2-inch piece hot chili pepper, or ¼ teaspoon red
    pepper flakes
1 small clove garlic minced
½ teaspoon salt
⅛ teaspoon freshly ground pepper
1½ cups heavy cream
2 tablespoons minced broadleaf parsley

In a heavy skillet combine the tomatoes, vodka, chili pepper, garlic, salt, and pepper. Cook over high heat, stirring constantly, until almost all the liquid has evaporated, about 6 to 8 minutes. Add the cream and bring the sauce to a boil. Continue to boil the sauce, uncovered, until it is reduced by one-third (about 15 minutes). Keep warm until ready to serve, then stir in the parsley.
Makes 2 cups. Preparation time: 30 minutes

 # WHITE WINE CREAM SAUCE
Salsa di Panna e Vino

This velvety rich wine sauce is so quick and easy to prepare that I often rely on it when guests arrive unexpectedly. I usually serve it tossed with spinach fettucine or linguine and served with a fresh green salad, or poured over blanched tender asparagus or broccoli. In place of dry white wine, you may substitute a frutier wine or even a sparkling Asti Spumante for a champagne sauce. Due to its richness, this cream sauce should be portioned with discretion.

1 cup dry white wine
2 cups heavy cream
½ teaspoon salt
A pinch of freshly ground white pepper

Bring the wine to a boil in an enameled or stainless steel saucepan and allow to reduce by half, about 5 to 8 minutes. Stir in the cream and gently bring to a boil, whisking frequently to ensure the sauce does not boil over. Continue to cook for 2 minutes, then season with salt and pepper and serve immediately.
Yield: 1½ cups. Preparation time: 10 minutes

GARLIC MAYONNAISE
Maionese all'Aglio

Although this mayonnaise can be made by hand with a whisk, you may need to add more egg yolk to absorb the oil. A blender or food processor makes a lighter sauce because of the speed with which the oil is emulsified into the yolk. Use a paler, milder tasting oil for this recipe.

1 egg yolk
1 garlic clove, minced
½ teaspoon tomato paste
Grated rind of 1 orange, orange part only
1 tablespoon lemon juice
½ teaspoon salt
¼ teaspoon freshly ground white pepper
½ to ¾ cup olive oil

Combine all the ingredients except the oil in a blender or food processor and blend thoroughly. With the food processor running, slowly add ½ cup of oil in a thin stream, making sure all the oil is emulsified before adding more. In a blender, add 2 tablespoons of oil, blend well, and repeat until ½ cup has been used. If the mayonnaise looks shiny at an early stage, stop adding oil for a few seconds but continue to blend until the mayonnaise is smooth and homogeneous. After adding the first ½ cup of oil, check the consistency of the mayonnaise and add more oil only as necessary. Use immediately, or cover and refrigerate for up to one week.
Makes 1 cup. Preparation time: 10 minutes

BÉCHAMEL
Balsamella

The provenance of this classic white sauce is a matter of dispute between the Italians and the French. But whatever its origin, it certainly makes an important contribution to both cuisines. Béchamel is so versatile and variable that it can be the base for other sauces, used to thicken and flavor soups, and it works well as a binding agent in molded dishes and lasagne. For the onion and cheese sauces which follow, it forms a creamy base enabling them to be served with pastas, parboiled vegetables, or polenta dishes with equal success.

The basic sauce is made of butter, flour, and milk. Once the technique of preparing béchamel is mastered, the sauce is quickly and easily made. After adding the flour to the butter, the mixture is briefly cooked to eliminate some of the raw taste of the flour. Heating the flour also makes it more receptive to the swelling process that occurs when the liquid is absorbed.

The two most common problems with white sauces such as béchamel are lumping and burning. Lumping may be avoided by pouring a cold liquid into the hot *roux* (the flour and butter paste) and whisking almost constantly while it comes to a boil. Though many references suggest using hot liquid, I find that the sauce then siezes too quickly, resulting in a mixture riddled with hard lumps. To avoid burning, whisk constantly over medium heat to keep the flour from sticking to the pan bottom, and use a heavy-bottomed saucepan if you can.

BÉCHAMEL
Balsamella

¼ cup butter
¼ cup flour
2 cups cold milk
1 teaspoon salt
¼ teaspoon freshly ground white pepper
A dash of freshly grated nutmeg

In a heavy 1-quart saucepan, melt the butter and remove the pan from the heat. Whisk in the flour and when the mixture is smooth, return to medium heat. Cook the *roux*, whisking constantly, until the foam subsides and the flour begins to turn golden. Slowly add the milk and continue to cook, whisking frequently, until the sauce comes to a boil, about 10 minutes. Season with salt, pepper, and nutmeg. Allow the sauce to simmer gently for 10 minutes.

If you are not using the sauce immediately, dot the top with butter to keep a crust from forming. To store, pour the sauce into a container, cover the top with plastic wrap, cool, and refrigerate or freeze.
Makes 2 cups. Preparation time: 30 minutes

 # ONION BÉCHAMEL
Balsamella di Cipolla

¼ cup butter

1 cup finely chopped onion

¼ cup flour

2 cups cold milk

1 teaspoon salt

¼ teaspoon freshly ground white pepper

A dash of freshly grated nutmeg

In a heavy 1-quart saucepan, melt the butter and gently sauté the onion until golden, about 5 minutes. Whisk in the flour and continue to cook over medium heat for 3 minutes, whisking frequently. Add the milk and bring the sauce to a boil, whisking frequently. Season with salt, pepper, and nutmeg and simmer for 10 minutes, whisking often. The sauce should be thick enough to coat the back of a spoon; add milk or cook further to correct the consistency. To store the sauce, see Béchamel, above.
Makes 3 cups. Preparation time: 30 minutes

 # CHEESE BÉCHAMEL
Salsa di Formaggio

¼ cup butter

¼ cup flour

2 cups cold milk

½ teaspoon salt

¼ teaspoon freshly ground white pepper

⅛ teaspoon freshly grated nutmeg

1 cup freshly grated Italian fontina

½ cup freshly grated parmesan

In a heavy 1-quart saucepan, melt the butter; remove the pan from the heat, and whisk in the flour. Cook over medium heat, whisking frequently, for 5 minutes. Add the milk and season with salt, pepper, and nutmeg. Whisking frequently, bring the sauce to a boil and simmer for 10 minutes. Just before serving, check for consistency; the mixture should coat the back of a spoon. If necessary, thin the sauce with milk or water. Stir in the cheeses and serve as soon as they have melted into the sauce.

Makes 3 cups. Preparation time: 30 minutes

GORGONZOLA SAUCE
Salsa di Gorgonzola

Gorgonzola is one of the creamiest of the blue cheeses, and it is this softness that makes it ideal for adding to sauces. But its richness and strong, savory flavor mean that this sauce should be used with care. A good fresh pasta is sometimes all that is needed to accompany it, perhaps with some tender fresh peas to add color and texture.

1 recipe Béchamel (Page 51)

⅔ cup crumbled gorgonzola

⅓ cup heavy cream

1 tablespoon butter

⅔ cup chopped toasted hazelnuts or walnuts

Bring the béchamel sauce to a simmer. Whisk in the cheese, heavy cream, and butter. When the cheese has melted and the sauce is smooth, stir in half the nuts. Serve immediately, garnishing the dish with the remaining nuts.

Makes 3 cups. Preparation time: 40 minutes

PESTO SAUCES

In Italian pesto means "pounded" and can refer to a multitude of sauces which grace not only pasta but also hot and cold vegetables, salad greens, and dishes made with rice and other grains; or which can be stirred into a hot soup at tableside as aromatic enrichment. Although the classic *Pesto alla Genovese* is best known, with its combination of fresh basil, garlic, olive oil, pine nuts, and parmesan or pecorino, a pesto can be based on any of a number of fresh herbs including tarragon, sage, oregano, and broadleaf parsley. Equally, olive oil can give way to the more subtle and elegant butter and cream; pine nuts can be replaced by walnuts, hazelnuts, or even the sweeter almond; and any hard Italian cheese can be freshly grated into the sauce.

Historically, pesto is made with a mortar and pestle, and the time and energy this requires is certainly well spent, since the flavors more often than not seem to be richer and the texture smoother. Modern blenders and food processors, however, simplify matters with admirable results.

Pesto freezes well and this is an ideal way to capture the aromas of the fresh herbs of summer for winter months. If you plan to freeze the sauce, omit the cheese and add it immediately before use. Because of the richness of these sauces, they should be used with discretion; one cup will serve six.

 BASIL PESTO
Pesto alla Genovese

This basil sauce from the Ligurian capital is the mother of all the pesto sauces. Traditionally, it is served with the local version of ribbon noodles, trenette, which are similar to fettucine.

1 tablespoon pine nuts
½ cup olive oil, preferably extra virgin
2 to 3 garlic cloves, minced
½ teaspoon salt
1 cup tightly packed fresh basil leaves
¼ cup freshly grated pecorino

Combine the pine nuts, olive oil, garlic, and salt in a blender or food processor and chop finely. Add the basil and continue to chop, using a pulse or turning the machine on and off, scraping down the sides of the container occasionally. When the basil is just chopped, not puréed, spoon the mixture into a bowl and stir in the cheese. Serve at room temperature.

Makes 1 cup. Preparation time: 15 minutes

 # FRESH HERB SAUCE
Salsa Verde

Italian green sauces are uncooked, piquant mixtures of fresh herbs and vinegars. Traditionally, hard-cooked eggs were used to help bind the mixture, but our blenders and food processors are very good at emulsifying vinaigrette sauces. Any combination of green herbs may be used, although I particularly like this pairing of sweet basil and tart tarragon.

½ cup tightly packed fresh basil leaves

½ cup tightly packed fresh parsley leaves

2 tablespoons fresh tarragon leaves

½ cup chopped scallions, green and white parts

2 tablespoons small capers, rinsed and drained

1 garlic clove, minced

1 teaspoon salt

½ teaspoon freshly ground pepper

¼ cup white wine vinegar

½ cup olive oil, preferably extra virgin

Chop all the dry ingredients together by hand or in a blender or food processor, scraping down frequently. Add the vinegar, then the oil, with a whisk or by pouring them into your machine with the blade running. Mix well with a whisk just before serving. Use immediately or cover and refrigerate for up to a week. Serve at room temperature.

Makes 1½ cups.   Preparation time: 10 minutes by machine, 25 minutes by hand

TARRAGON CREAM PESTO
Pesto di Dragoncello alla Crema

1 cup fresh tarragon leaves
2 garlic cloves, minced
½ teaspoon salt
½ cup pine nuts
1 cup fresh breadcrumbs
2 tablespoons lemon juice
½ cup olive oil
½ cup heavy cream
¼ cup warm water
¼ cup toasted pine nuts, for garnish

Combine the tarragon, garlic, and salt in a blender or food processor and chop coarsely, scraping the container to mix. Add the pine nuts and chop finely. Add the breadcrumbs and lemon juice and continue to mix, pausing to scrape down the sides of the container. If you're using a food processor, with the machine running pour the oil in through the feed tube in a slow stream, then add the cream and warm water, scraping and turning the mixture after each addition to ensure that the sauce is homogeneous. For a blender, add small amounts of the oil, cream, and finally the water, mixing well after each addition. Serve immediately or cover and refrigerate for up to 2 hours. Serve the sauce at room temperature, garnished with toasted pine nuts.
Makes 2 cups. Preparation time: 20 minutes

DRIED MUSHROOM SAUCE
Salsa di Porcini Secchi

¾ cup grappa, brandy, or scotch

2 ounces dried *porcini* or ½ pound fresh mushrooms·

2 tablespoons butter, if using fresh mushrooms

2 tablespoons finely chopped shallots

¾ teaspoon salt

⅛ teaspoon freshly ground pepper

½ cup heavy cream

1 cup butter, cut into 16 tablespoons, at room
    temperature

2 tablespoons finely chopped broadleaf parsley

If using *porcini,* bring the liquor to boil in a heavy 2-quart saucepan and add the mushrooms. Remove the pan from the heat and allow to steep for 15 minutes. Remove the mushrooms and chop them, then return to the pan. For fresh mushrooms, wipe them with a damp cloth and cut in small dice. Melt the 2 tablespoons butter in the saucepan and sauté the mushrooms briefly, then add the liquor.

Add the shallots to the mushroom mixture and season with salt and pepper. Simmer until the liquid has almost evaporated. Add the cream and reduce by half, about 10 minutes. (The addition of cream helps to stabilize the sauce.) Over low heat, add the butter by tablespoon, swirling each in with a whisk and allowing it to liquefy before adding another. Regulate the heat so that the butter is emulsified without melting into butterfat. It may be necessary to remove the pan from the heat at intervals to ensure that it does not overheat—the sauce separates if allowed to come to a boil. When all the butter has been incorporated, stir in the parsley. Serve immediately or if necessary, place the saucepan in a bowl of warm water until ready to serve.

Makes 1½ cups. Preparation time: 30 minutes

MARSALA MUSHROOM SAUCE
Salsa di Funghi alla Marsala

This sauce is best quickly sautéed at the last minute so that the fresh mushrooms retain their texture and do not become rubbery. Serve with rice dishes or on its own as a hot antipasto or vegetable side dish.

1 pound white, tightly closed mushrooms
Juice of 1 lemon
2 tablespoons vegetable oil
¼ cup minced shallots
1 teaspoon salt
¼ teaspoon freshly ground pepper
½ cup Marsala
1 cup butter, cut into 16 tablespoons, at room
    temperature

Clean the mushrooms with a damp cloth, cut into thin slices, and toss with the lemon juice. In a heavy skillet, heat the oil until almost smoking. Add the mushrooms and sauté quickly, shaking the pan and turning the mushrooms with a wooden spoon until lightly browned. Add the shallots, season with salt and pepper, and sauté for 1 minute, shaking and stirring. Transfer the mushrooms to a bowl and return the pan to the heat. Immediately pour in the Marsala and reduce heat to medium. With the wooden spoon, loosen and scrape up the brown bits in the bottom of the pan. When the wine has reduced to about 2 tablespoons, turn the heat to low and begin to add the butter. Swirl each tablespoon in with a whisk, removing the pan from the heat if it gets too hot and the butter begins to melt. (The butter should be emulsified into the wine so that the sauce has a creamy consistency. If the mixture is allowed to boil, the butterfat will break down into a clear liquid.) Keep swirling in the butter, piece by piece, until it has all been added, then immediately return the mushrooms to the pan, along with any liquid that has accumulated in the bowl. Stir and toss the mushrooms in the butter and immediately sauce the dish you are serving or transfer to a heated sauceboat. Serve at once.
Makes 2 cups. Preparation time: 25 minutes

CHAPTER 5

PASTA

Pasta is a cornerstone of the Italian diet and hardly a day goes by without it being included in a meal. Although slurred in the past as a fattening filler, pasta is being appreciated more in the United States as an elegant and valuable source of protein in its fresh and shapely forms. Freshly made pasta is softer and more delicately flavored than store-bought. Making pasta at home enables you to add herbs and spices to the dough, adding even more variations in flavor and color. Like bread, the best pasta is made by hand and enjoyed within hours, when these subtle qualities are freshest and most pronounced.

Hand-made pasta takes time, patience, and perserverence to roll the dough thin enough so that it doesn't become a thick mass when added to a pot of boiling water. Manual machines are fairly inexpensive and simplify the process. Electric machines, once mastered, make the job even easier and enable you to make round and tubular pastas such as spaghetti and ziti.

The cooking time for fresh pasta is a fraction of that for dry macaroni and so you should test it often to determine the exact moment when it is tender but still firm to the bite—*al dente.* Before you begin, read the directions in Egg Pasta (Page 60) for fresh pasta making, cooking, and storing. Stores specializing in fresh gourmet foods often carry fresh pastas and these are a good substitute when you don't have the time to prepare your own.

Dried, store-bought pastas do have their merits. Italian durum wheat pastas are being imported to this country under many brands and in a myriad of shapes and sizes impossible to produce at home without an electric pasta machine. The new American high protein blended pastas, which use soy flour to complement the protein of wheat flour and health food pastas using whole wheat and Jerusalem artichoke flour are excellent meat substitutes, with as much texture as the Italian product but quite a different flavor.

59

EGG PASTA
Pasta all 'Uovo

This recipe provides the basic instructions and techniques for making pasta at home, whether by hand or with a manual or electric pasta machine. The same techniques apply to all the flavored pasta recipes which follow. These quantities will serve 6.

3 cups flour, approximately

4 eggs

1 teaspoon salt

4 teaspoons milk (optional, for stuffed pastas)

By hand: Place the flour in a mound on a large (24 by 36-inch) wooden board or countertop, preferably not marble. Make a well in the center and put the eggs, salt, and optional milk into it. Mix the eggs with a fork and then begin to blend in the flour, taking it from the sides of the well. When the dough is too thick to stir with the fork, work in the remaining flour with your hands, until the dough is no longer sticky and can be gathered into a ball. Depending on the humidity and the flour, the dough may not absorb all the flour. Reserve any left over for kneading and rolling out. If all the flour has been added and the dough is still sticky, add more while kneading to produce a smooth, dry, elastic dough.

Begin to knead the dough, pushing into it with the heel of your hand and folding over with your fingers. Rotate the dough a quarter turn as you work to be sure it is being evenly mixed and continue to knead for 10 minutes. Then cover the dough with a clean towel or ceramic bowl and allow it to rest for at least 20 minutes.

Clean the work surface to ready for rolling out. While you can use a heavy, rotating rolling pin, the best tool for this is a long, thin rolling pin about 30-inches long and 2 to 3-inches thick. Such pins are generally available at good cooking equipment stores, or you can have one made out of hardwood at a lumber yard. (If you do have one made, sand it thoroughly and wash well before using.) Divide the dough in half and roll out each individually. As you work the first half, cover the other with a cloth or bowl to keep it from drying out. Lightly flour your work surface and place the pasta dough in front of you. Starting from the center, roll out, pushing the dough forward and down. Rotate the dough a quarter turn and repeat the rolling. (The turning stretches different parts of the dough and keeps it from sticking to the work surface.) Flour the surface as necessary, and continue to

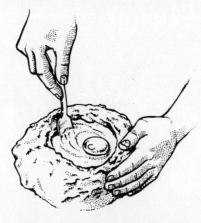

1 Place the eggs, salt, and milk (optional) in a well formed by the flour. Mix with a fork, pulling the flour in from the sides of the well.

2 When the dough is too stiff to work with a fork, gather it up and work in the remaining flour with your hands.

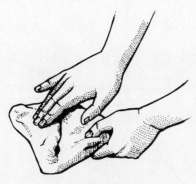

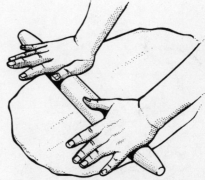

3 Knead the dough using the heel of your hand then fold over the edges with your fingers. Continue kneading, rotating the dough as you work, for about 10 minutes.

4 Let the dough rest for at least 20 minutes. Roll out on a lightly floured surface starting at the center and pushing the dough forward and down. Turn the dough a quarter turn each time and continue to roll to the desired thickness.

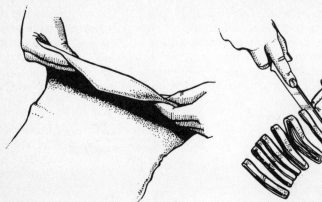

1 Allow the dough to dry for 20-30 minutes then fold it into a flat roll about 3-4 inches wide.

2 Holding the dough gently, cut into strips with a sharp knife to the desired width. Separate the noodles and allow to dry on a clean towel or rack for about 10 minutes before cooking.

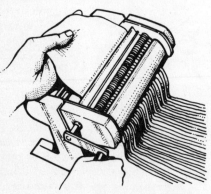

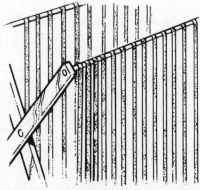

1 With a manual pasta machine, select the setting and feed in a sheet at a time, supporting the emerging noodles with your free hand.

2 Separate the cut noodles and allow to dry on a clean towel or rack for about 10 minutes before cooking.

roll and turn. When the pasta is fairly thin, roll it onto the pin and as you roll it out against the surface, stretch it widthwise with your hands. Turn the dough over and repeat the process. Continue to stretch the dough in this way until the desired thickness is reached. Lasagne and stuffed pastas are ¹⁄₁₆-inch thick; fettucine and other noodles are slightly thinner and require more rolling. The dough is ready when it is almost translucent: against the light, the shadow of your hand should show through.

Allow the dough to rest and dry, 10 minutes for stuffed pastas, 15 for others, before cutting. For the filled pastas, cut the flat sheets according to the directions in the recipe you are preparing. To cut long, broad, or flat noodles, roll up the pasta sheet and slice it in even measures with a sharp knife. Unroll and separate the strands to dry. After the pasta is cut, it should be dried for at least an additional 10 minutes before cooking.

Preparation time: 1 hour, approximately. Yield: 1 lb. (about six servings)

By food processor: Place the flour and salt in the work bowl. Lightly beat the eggs (and optional milk) in a separate bowl and add gradually to the flour through the feed tube with the machine running. When the dough has formed a ball, turn the machine off and check for consistency. If some of the dough is still dry and flaky, add a little beaten egg through the feed tube and work into the dough. If it is sticky, turn it out onto the work surface to knead in flour, tablespoon by tablespoon, by hand. If the dough is dry and smooth when you turn it out onto the work surface, knead it briefly to see if it is evenly mixed. If so, knead the dough for 5 minutes then knead and roll out the dough by hand (described above) or with a manual pasta machine.

Preparation time for food processor dough: 20 minutes

By manual pasta machine: To knead the pasta, set the machine at its widest setting. Make the dough by hand as described above, then divide the dough into quarters and keep covered with a cloth or bowl while working with each portion. Flatten one quarter and feed it into the machine, turning the handle in an even motion. When the dough has been rolled through the first time, fold it in thirds and press it together to release any air bubbles. Repeat the rolling process, turning the dough so that an unfolded end is fed into the machine, with the machine still at its widest setting. Lightly flour the machine, if necessary. Roll the dough through at the widest setting, folding and turning it each time, a total of eight times.

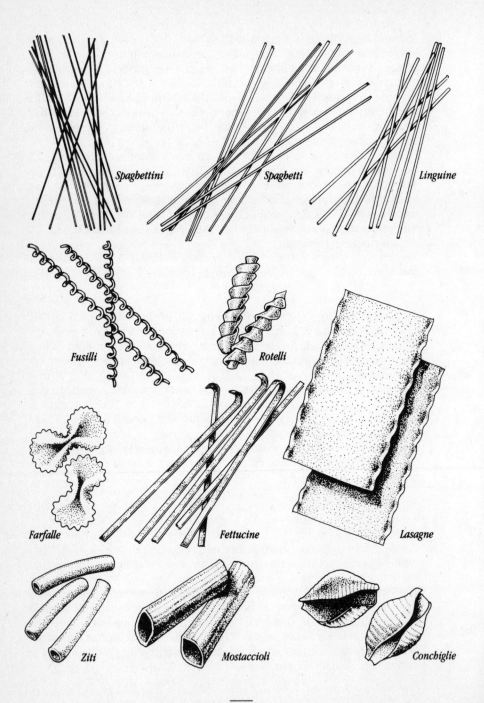

Spaghettini

Spaghetti

Linguine

Fusilli

Rotelli

Farfalle

Fettucine

Lasagne

Ziti

Mostaccioli

Conchiglie

Check the dough for elasticity. If it shrinks easily when stretched or handled, allow it to rest for 20 minutes, covered with a cloth. But if the dough doesn't seem elastic, proceed with the rolling out. Reset the pasta machine at the second widest setting and feed the dough, unfolded, through once at this setting. Continue to feed the dough through each time at a progressively thinner setting. The dough will come out in longer sheets with each new setting. At wide sections in the strip, stretch the dough so that it doesn't flatten sideways. This will help to produce a uniform width to the sheet.

Use an even hand to rotate the machine handle, and work at the speed which is most comfortable. But as you gain experience, try to increase the speed with which you roll out the dough. Working quickly keeps the gluten strands from overdeveloping and making the pasta rubbery.

For lasagne and filled pastas, the sheet should be rolled only to the next to last setting. For fettucine, roll the dough to the thinnest setting. On a lightly floured surface, cut the pasta sheets into workable pieces, about 12-inches long. Allow the dough to dry for 10 minutes, then layer the sheets with clean cloths or paper towels to keep them moist. Cut each sheet individually as required for your recipe. Most manual machines have a cutting attachment, and the pasta is generally fed in as it is for rolling. Consult the manufacturer's directions for more detail.

Preparation time 20–45 minutes

By electric pasta machine: Unlike manual machines, electric pastamakers can make fresh spaghetti and a variety of round and tubular pasta shapes as well as gnocchi. If you are using one, follow the quantities and instruction provided by the manufacturer. Use the measuring utensils included with the machine for best results, and take care not to overknead the dough. Dust the finished pasta with cornmeal to keep the strands from sticking together.

Preparation time: 20–30 minutes

Cooking the pasta: To cook pasta properly, use a big pot with lots of salted, rapidly boiling water. For the recipes in this book, you'll need about 8 quarts of water and 2 tablespoons of salt. The pasta should be added when the water is at a rolling boil, just after stirring in the salt. Stir the pasta at once with a wooden spoon, then stir several times more during the cooking. The only sure method to know when the pasta is cooked *al dente*, or firm to the bite, is by tasting it. Test often to catch the moment when it is cooked, drain quickly, and add the sauce. The thinner and fresher the pasta, the less time it will take to cook. Thicker, drier, or filled pastas need longer cooking. Rinse the pasta only if it is to be used for lasagne or cannelloni or dishes in which it is layered, filled, and baked.

To store: Toss the cut pasta with semolina or cornmeal if you are not using it immediately, or if you are freezing or drying it, to keep the strands from sticking together. Allow the noodles to dry on a rack or lightly floured surface. You may want to dry them completely and store for future use. For a softer, more flavorful noodle, freeze the pasta while it is still fresh. Form little nests in portion sizes and freeze them on a baking sheet. When frozen, transfer carefully to a plastic bag, seal, and return to the freezer.

 ## SEMOLINA PASTA

Semolina is a hard durum wheat flour in granular form, available in Italian groceries and natural food stores. It is higher in protein and gluten content than all-purpose flour, and is easier to work with for pasta making. This grain makes a somewhat heavier pasta that stands up well to robust dishes such as Spaghetti with Eggplant and Tomatoes (Page 70).

2 cups semolina
1 egg
2 tablespoons extra virgin olive oil
½ teaspoon salt
¼ cup warm water

Use the semolina as you would flour, following the recipe for Egg Pasta on Page 60.

 ## BASIL PASTA

2 teaspoons olive oil, preferably extra virgin
1 garlic clove, minced

¼ cup minced fresh basil
3½ cups flour, approximately
4 to 5 eggs
½ teaspoon salt

Heat the oil and sauté the garlic for 1 minute. Remove from the heat and stir in the basil. Follow the general directions in Egg Pasta (Page 60), adding the herbs to the flour well with the eggs and salt.

 # CHILI PEPPER PASTA

2 teaspoons olive oil
1 small garlic clove, minced
2 tablespoons minced hot chili pepper
3½ cups flour, approximately
4 to 5 eggs
½ teaspoon salt

Heat the oil and lightly sauté the garlic. Remove from the heat and stir in the minced chili pepper. Follow the directions for Egg Pasta (Page 60), adding the pepper oil with the eggs and salt.

 # BUCKWHEAT PASTA

1½ cups buckwheat flour
¾ cup flour
2 eggs
1 tablespoon milk
1 tablespoon water
½ teaspoon salt

Combine the flours and make the pasta following the basic recipe on Page 60. Buckwheat flour makes a soft dough best kneaded by hand. If you do knead by machine, do not turn the pasta sheet around after folding; simply feed it into the machine folded side first.

SPINACH PASTA

This pliable dough is easy to roll out because of the water content of the spinach. For the same reason, it does take a little longer to dry before cutting and cooking. It may help to sprinkle the rolled dough with a bit of semolina or cornmeal to cut its dampness. The deep green color of the pasta is beautiful when contrasted with cream sauces and layered in lasagnes or pasta rolls.

¾ pound fresh spinach, thoroughly washed, or
    ½ 10-ounce package frozen spinach
2½ cups flour, approximately
2 to 3 eggs
½ teaspoon salt

Cook the spinach in the water clinging to its leaves in a covered saucepan over high heat until just wilted, stirring once, or thaw frozen spinach. Squeeze the excess moisture from the spinach and mince it. Follow the directions for Egg Pasta (Page 60), mixing the spinach, eggs, and salt in the flour well.

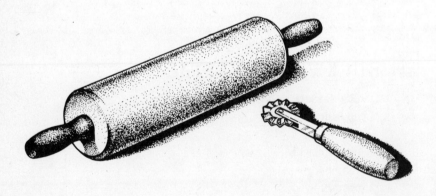

SPAGHETTINI WITH GARLIC, OIL, AND GINGER
Spaghettini Aglio e Olio

Adding fresh ginger to the classic combination of spaghetti, olive oil, and garlic gives this dish a distinctive and interesting flavor.

1 recipe Egg Pasta (Page 60), or 1½ pounds dry
   spaghettini
¾ cup olive oil, preferably extra virgin
1 tablespoon minced fresh ginger root
3 garlic cloves, minced
¼ cup minced broadleaf parsley
1½ tablespoons salt
⅛ teaspoon freshly ground pepper

Cut the pasta into linguine and allow to dry for 15 minutes. Heat ⅔ cup olive oil in a skillet or small saucepan, until a drop of water will sizzle in it. Stir in the ginger, garlic, and parsley, and remove the pan from the heat. Season the oil with ½ tsp. of salt and pepper and allow the mixture to steep as you prepare the pasta. Bring several quarts of water to a boil and stir in the remaining salt. Carefully add the pasta and stir in the remaining olive oil. Cook the pasta until *al dente*, testing frequently. Drain immediately and toss with the sauce.
Serves 6. Preparation time: 30 minutes

CHILI PEPPER LINGUINE
Linguine al Peperoncino

1 recipe Chili Pepper Pasta (Page 67)
½ cup olive oil, preferably extra virgin
1 garlic clove, minced
½ teaspoon salt
⅛ teaspoon freshly ground pepper
1 cup minced broadleaf parsley
½ cup freshly grated pecorino romano (optional)

Cut the pasta into linguine, and allow to dry on a rack or floured surface for at least 15 minutes. Heat the olive oil in a small saucepan until it is very hot, so that a drop of water will sizzle immediately in it. Add the garlic, remove from the heat and season with salt and pepper. Stir the pasta into several quarts of salted boiling water and cook until *al dente*. Depending on the freshness of the pasta, this will take only 30 seconds to 2 minutes, so test frequently. Drain and toss with the garlic oil and parsley. Serve with grated cheese if desired.
Serves 6. Preparation time: 30 minutes

SPAGHETTI WITH EGGPLANT AND TOMATOES
Spaghetti con Melanzane e Pomodori

4 small eggplants, peeled and sliced ½-inch thick

1 teaspoon salt

1 recipe Semolina Pasta (Page 66) or 2 pounds
 dry spaghetti

¾ cup olive oil

2 garlic cloves, minced

2 pounds plum tomatoes or 2 32-ounce cans
 plum tomatoes, drained, peeled, seeded, and
 coarsely chopped

Salt to taste

Freshly ground pepper to taste

1 tablespoon finely chopped fresh basil

½ cup freshly grated pecorino romano

Sprinkle the eggplant with salt and allow it to drain, weighted with a plate or cutting board, on paper towels for 30 minutes. If you are using semolina pasta, cut it into spaghetti and allow it to dry for 15 minutes. Heat ¼ cup of the olive oil in a large skillet and sauté the eggplant over medium-high heat until brown on both sides. Drain on paper towels. Heat the remaining oil and sauté the garlic until golden. Add the tomatoes and cook for 15 minutes, until the juices have evaporated, stirring occasionally. Add salt, pepper, and the basil. Stir in the eggplant and keep the sauce hot while you cook the spaghetti. Stir the spaghetti into salted boiling water and cook to *al dente*. Drain and toss with the sauce; sprinkle with grated cheese.
Serves 6. Preparation time: 45 minutes

BUCKWHEAT PASTA SALAD WITH SAVOY CABBAGE
Insalata di Pasta all'Orzo con Covolo Cappuccio

1 recipe Buckwheat Pasta (Page 67)
1½ cups Cold Tomato Sauce (Page 48)
1 medium savoy cabbage, cut in strips ¼-inch wide and
   3-inches long
½ cup freshly grated parmesan (optional)

Cut the pasta into ¼-inch fettucine and allow to dry for at least 20 minutes. Cook the pasta in several quarts of salted boiling water to *al dente* (1 to 3 minutes, depending on its freshness) testing frequently. Drain and toss the hot pasta with the sauce and cabbage. Serve hot or at room temperature with or without grated cheese.
Serves 6. Preparation time: 40 minutes

FETTUCINE WITH SUMMER VEGETABLES
Fettucine in Salsa di Ortaggi

This easy, quick, and refreshing dish is wonderful in the summer when fresh produce abounds and time in the kitchen should be kept to a minimum. Choose only vegetables that are perfectly ripe.

1 recipe Egg Pasta (Page 60)
2 medium zucchini, well scrubbed, in ½-inch dice
5 or 6 plum tomatoes, or 2 large tomatoes, peeled,
   seeded, in ½-inch dice
8 paper-thin slices red onion, divided into rings
3 tablespoons minced broadleaf parsley
1 tablespoon minced fresh mint
1 garlic clove, minced
½ cup olive oil, preferably extra virgin
3 tablespoons Balsamic or red wine vinegar

1 teaspoon salt

⅛ teaspoon freshly ground pepper

¼ cup freshly grated parmesan (optional)

Cut the pasta to ¼-inch fettucine and allow to dry. Combine the zucchini, tomatoes, onion, parsley, mint, garlic, oil, and vinegar in a mixing bowl. Season with salt and pepper. Stir the fettucine into salted boiling water and cook until just *al'dente*, testing often. Quickly drain the pasta and toss it with the vegetables. Serve hot, with grated cheese, or allow to cool and serve at room temperature.
Serves 6. Preparation time: 15 minutes

GREEN BEANS, POTATOES, AND PASTA WITH PESTO
Fagiolini Verde, Patate e Pasta con Pesto

½ pound green beans, cut in ¾-inch pieces

¾ pound new or red potatoes

1½ cups dry tubetti or penne

1 recipe Basil Pesto (Page 54)

½ teaspoon freshly ground pepper

2 tablespoons Balsamic or red wine vinegar (optional)

Steam the green beans over salted water or blanch them in lots of salted water for 2 to 3 minutes, just until tender. Refresh immediately in cold water; when cool, drain and set aside. Cook the potatoes in salted boiling water until tender, 20 to 30 minutes depending on their size. When the potatoes are almost done, bring the pasta water to a boil. Salt the water and stir in the pasta. Drain the potatoes and cool slightly. As the pasta cooks, peel the potatoes and cut into ¾-inch dice. Toss with half the pesto and reserve. Cook the macaroni until *al dente*, testing frequently. As soon as it is done, drain and toss with the remaining pesto. Add the green beans, potatoes, and pepper. Toss the vegetables together and serve at once. This dish is also very tasty served cold. Allow it to come to room temperature, tossing occasionally, then cover and chill. Mix in the vinegar just before serving.
Serves 6. Preparation time: 45 minutes

GREEK SICILIAN SALAD
Insalata Greco Siciliana

When served cold, pasta should be slightly undercooked so that it will be firm and fresh after marinating for several hours. In this recipe, the pasta is given a subtle flavor by cooking it with garlic and lemon rind; tie these together in a cheesecloth bag so that they can be easily removed after cooking. This salad will be ready after 1 or 2 hours marinating; if it is kept longer than that, squeeze the juice of half a lemon over the top to freshen it.

1 lemon
5 garlic cloves, peeled and crushed
1 pound rotelli or conchiglie
½ cup olive oil
¼ cup freshly grated pecorino romano
½ cup chopped broadleaf parsley
1 teaspoon chopped oregano
¾ cup plum tomatoes, peeled, seeded, in ½-inch dice
1 cup ricotta salata, in ½-inch dice
½ cup pitted and sliced Greek olives

Grate the lemon rind and tie it and 4 crushed garlic cloves in a cheesecloth bag. Put the bag in several quarts of salted boiling water and stir in the pasta. Cook the pasta until it is tender but still quite firm. Meanwhile, prepare a large bowl for the salad by rubbing the inside with the remaining crushed garlic clove. When the pasta is done, remove the cheesecloth bag and drain the pasta, then transfer to the salad bowl. Pour in the olive oil and mix well. Sprinkle on the grated cheese and continue to mix, adding the parsley and oregano. Add the tomatoes, the ricotta salata, and the olives, and toss the salad to mix evenly. Juice the lemon and sprinkle over the salad. Marinate at room temperature for 1 to 2 hours, tossing occasionally.
Serves 6. Preparation time (not including marinating): 30 minutes

TAGLIATELLE WITH GORGONZOLA SAUCE
Tagliatelle al Gorgonzola

1 recipe Egg Pasta (Page 60), or 2 pounds dry tagliatelle
1 recipe Gorgonzola Sauce (Page 53)
⅔ cup coarsely chopped toasted, peeled hazelnuts

Roll out the pasta and cut into ¼-inch noodles. Allow these to dry for 15 minutes. Make or reheat the sauce. Cook the tagliatelle in salted boiling water to *al dente*. Fresh noodles will cook in less than a minute, so test almost immediately. Drain the pasta and toss with half the sauce; sprinkle the toasted hazelnuts over it, and pass the additional sauce separately.
Serves 6. Preparation time: 25 minutes

 # FETTUCINE IN CHICK PEA SAUCE
Fettucine e Ceci

½ cup olive oil
1 cup chopped onion
1 garlic clove, minced
2 tablespoons minced fresh basil or 1 tablespoon
    minced fresh rosemary
2 tablespoons tomato paste
1 teaspoon salt
⅛ teaspoon freshly ground pepper
2 cups dried chick peas soaked in water overnight, or
    2 16-ounce cans chick peas
1 recipe Semolina Pasta (Page 66) or 1 pound dry
    fettucine
½ cup freshly grated parmesan

Heat the olive oil in a large skillet and gently sauté the onion until golden, about 5 minutes. Add the garlic, fresh herb, and tomato paste, and season with salt and pepper. Stir in the chick peas and add water to cover. If you are using canned chick peas, do not drain them but

add extra water if necessary. Simmer until the chick peas are tender, about 1½ hours for dried and 30 minutes for canned. Cut the pasta into fettucine and allow to dry. When the chick peas are tender, purée half of them in their liquid. Return the purée to the pan and check for consistency, adding water as necessary to make a sauce that will coat the back of a spoon. Cook the pasta in salted boiling water until *al dente*. Drain and toss with the sauce; sprinkle with grated cheese.
Serves 6. Preparation time: 2 hours for dried chick peas; 1 hour for canned

HAY AND STRAW WITH CAPERS
Paglia e Fieno ai Capperi

The name 'hay and straw' is reminiscent of fields of freshly mown hay which, by baking in the sun, turns to straw. The green and yellow pastas are cooked and tossed together, mixing the two fresh colors.

½ recipe Egg Pasta (Page 60)

1 recipe Spinach Pasta (Page 68)

¼ cup small capers, rinsed and drained

½ cup black olives, pitted and sliced in thin rings

1 large garlic clove, minced

¼ teaspoon freshly ground pepper

1 cup butter

½ cup freshly grated pecorino romano (optional)

Cut the pasta into linguine and allow to dry. Combine the capers, olives, garlic, and pepper, and set aside. Melt the butter in a heavy saucepan over low heat. Cook until the foam disappears and it clarifies and begins to brown. As soon as the butter starts to brown, remove it from the heat and stir in the caper mixture. If the butter is browning too rapidly, pour it into a cool container; otherwise reserve it in the saucepan.

Stir the pasta into several quarts of salted boiling water. This pasta cooks very rapidly so test it almost immediately. As soon as the pasta is *al dente*, drain it and transfer to a warmed serving bowl or platter. Strain the butter over the pasta and toss to coat all the strands. Then sprinkle the capers, olives, and garlic mixture over the top and serve immediately, passing grated cheese if desired.
Serves 6. Preparation time: 40 minutes

FETTUCINE WITH ZUCCHINI NOODLES
Fettucine con Pasta di Zucchini

This recipe evolved while I was working on a series of low-calorie Italian dishes that would be quick enough to prepare on television. I liked the recipe so much that I've decided to include it here. The zucchini strips should resemble fettucine and are particularly attractive if one edge is accented with the green skin. If you are counting calories, substitute low-fat milk or half-and-half for the cream.

2 large zucchini

2 tablespoons olive oil

1 garlic clove, minced

1 cup ricotta

½ cup heavy cream

½ teaspoon freshly ground pepper

⅛ teaspoon nutmeg

1 recipe Egg Pasta (Page 60) cut to fettucine, or

    1 pound dry fettucine

¼ cup freshly grated pecorino romano or parmesan

2 tablespoons minced fresh basil or broadleaf parsley

Scrub the zucchini well but do not peel them. Using a vegetable peeler, cut off long, thin strips about ½-inch wide and the length of the zucchini.

Heat the oil in a large skillet and add the garlic. Sauté briefly, then add the zucchini strips and toss until slightly wilted. Remove from the heat and set aside.

Combine the ricotta and cream and season with salt, pepper, and nutmeg. Heat over a medium burner, whisking frequently, but do not allow the sauce to boil.

Bring to boil several quarts of water, add salt, then stir in the fettucine. Cook the pasta until just *al dente*, testing often. Whisk ½ cup of the pasta water into the cheese sauce. Drain the pasta and toss with the zucchini and sauce. Turn onto a warmed serving platter and sprinkle with the grated cheese and fresh herbs. Serve at once.
Serves 6. Preparation time (not including making pasta): 15 minutes

PASTA BOWS WITH SPRING VEGETABLES
Farfalle Primavera

Cooking the pasta and vegetables together in the same pot makes this version of pasta primavera a particularly quick and easy one. Dry pasta must be cooked longer than the vegetables, but with fresh pasta practically all the ingredients can be cooked together. For color I have chosen only green vegetables to toss with the white pasta and herb sauce, but vary the ingredients as you wish.

1 recipe Egg Pasta (Page 60), or 1½ pounds
    dry pasta bows
1½ cups Fresh Herb Sauce (Page 55)
1 cup mixed greens: spinach, escarole, curly endive,
    cut in ¼-inch strips
1 cup shelled fresh peas or frozen peas
2 cups small broccoli florets
2 cups sugar snap or snow peas, strings removed and
    halved on the diagonal
¾ cup freshly grated pecorino romano

Make the pasta in sheets and allow it to dry, covered with a clean cloth, for 10 minutes before cutting. Working with one sheet at a time, cut the pasta with a knife or fluted pasta wheel into rectangles 1½-inches long and ¾-inch wide. Squeeze each rectangle together in the center to form a little bow. Allow the bows to dry on a lightly floured surface for at least 15 minutes. Meanwhile, prepare the sauce and the vegetables. Allow the sauce to cool and combine with the leaf greens in a large serving dish and set aside
   Cook dry pasta in salted boiling water until it begins to soften, testing frequently. Stir in the fresh peas and cook for 3 minutes, then add the broccoli, sugar snap or snow peas, and return the water to boiling. If you are using frozen peas, add them with the other vegetables. With homemade pasta, cook the fresh peas for 3 minutes, then add the pasta and other vegetables at the same time. As soon as the pasta is *al dente,* drain and toss with the sauce and leaf greens and ¼ cup of the grated pecorino. Serve hot, passing the extra cheese. If you plan to have this dish at room temperature or chilled, do not add the cheese until just before serving. Allow the pasta to cool, tossing occasionally. *Serves 6. Preparation time (not including making pasta): 30 minutes*

RAVIOLI

Ravioli needs little introduction, and they are just sensational when freshly made. I often make a double quantity as it will keep for 2 weeks in the freezer. Freeze on a baking sheet first, then pack in a box with cornmeal sprinkled on each layer to prevent sticking. Do not defrost before cooking.

Filling:
2 eggs
1½ pounds ricotta
½ pound mozzarella, coarsely grated
¼ cup freshly grated parmesan
4 tablespoons chopped broadleaf parsley
½ teaspoon salt
⅛ teaspoon freshly ground pepper

Dough:
2¼ cups flour, approximately
3 eggs
½ teaspoon salt
3 teaspoons milk

Sauce:
2 cups Summer or Winter Tomato Sauce (Page 46)

For the filling, beat the eggs in a large bowl, then add the cheeses and parsley. Mix well, season with salt and pepper, and refrigerate until needed. Prepare the pasta following the directions on Page 60, rolling the dough in a rectangular shape ⅛-inch thick. Cut the sheet in half lengthwise. Set 1 piece aside, covered with a cloth or towel, and place the other on a lightly floured work surface. Drop teaspoons of the filling at evenly-spaced intervals of about 1½-inches across the sheet. Cover with the second sheet and press gently around each mound of filling to eliminate any air bubbles. Cut into squares with a pastry wheel or ravioli cutter and press the edges of each with the flat edge of the cutter to seal. (Alternatively, cut the ravioli with a knife and crimp the edges with the tines of a fork.) Allow to dry.

Make or reheat the sauce and simmer over low heat while the pasta cooks. Gently drop the ravioli, a few at a time, into salted rapidly boiling water. Cook them, stirring occasionally with a wooden spoon to prevent sticking, until they are *al dente*. This should take about 5 minutes after the water has returned to a boil. As soon as the ravioli are done, remove them with a skimmer or slotted spoon. Spoon over the sauce and serve at once.

Serves 6. Preparation time: 2 hours by hand, 1 with pasta machine

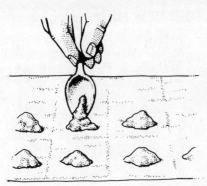

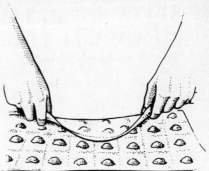

1 On one half of the rolled–out pasta drop teaspoons of the filling at regular, 1½-inch intervals.

2 When the dough is covered with mounds of filling, lay the second sheet of pasta on top.

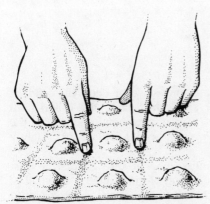

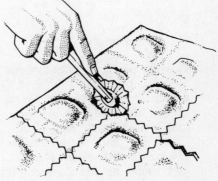

3 Press gently around each mound with your fingers to seal the two layers of dough and remove any air pockets.

4 Cut into squares using a pastry wheel or ravioli cutter. Separate and allow to dry for a few minutes before cooking.

SPINACH TORTELLINI WITH MIMOSA FILLING
Tortellini Verde Mimosa

Filling:

2 hard-cooked eggs

2 hard-cooked egg yolks

1 tablespoon butter

2 tablespoons finely chopped onion

½ cup ricotta

2 tablespoons freshly grated parmesan

2 tablespoons finely chopped broadleaf parsley

½ teaspoon salt

⅛ teaspoon freshly ground pepper

⅛ teaspoon nutmeg

Pasta:

2 recipes Spinach Pasta (Page 68)

2 teaspoons milk

Sauce:

1½ cups Béchamel (Page 51)

Pass the eggs and yolks through a coarse seive or chop them finely. Melt the butter in a small skillet and gently sauté the onion until golden, about 5 minutes. Transfer to a mixing bowl and stir in the cheeses and parsley, then season with salt, pepper, and nutmeg. Lightly fold in all the eggs and set aside.

Roll the pasta to ⅛-inch thickness and cut into rounds at least 2½-inches in diameter. Place ½ teaspoon of the filling on one half of each round. Brush the edges with milk and fold over the other half to make a crescent, pressing the edges to seal. Wrap the crescent lengthwise around your index finger and seal the 2 points, overlapping one point over the other. Place the finished tortellini on a rack or floured surface to dry and continue to shape the others. Allow to dry for at least 15 minutes, during which you can make or reheat the sauce. Then cook in salted boiling water until just *al dente*, about 3 to 5 minutes, testing frequently. Drain and toss with ½ cup of the sauce. Serve immediately. *Serves 6. Preparation time: 2¼ hours by hand, 1¼ with a pasta machine*

BASIL PASTA FILLED WITH SUN-DRIED TOMATOES
Cappelletti Basilico con Pomodori Secchi

These capelletti, or "little hats" can be made in various sizes; rich, sun-dried tomatoes are normally packed in olive oil and should be drained before using.

Filling:

2 ounces sun-dried tomatoes, in ¼-inch dice

½ cup ricotta

¼ cup freshly grated pecorino romano, or parmesan

1 garlic clove, minced

½ teaspoon salt

⅛ teaspoon freshly ground pepper

Pasta:

1 recipe Basil Pasta (Page 66)

2 teaspoons milk

Sauce:

½ cup butter, at room temperature

½ cup freshly grated pecorino romano, or parmesan

Mix together the ingredients for the filling and set aside. Roll the pasta to ⅛-inch thickness, and cut the sheets into 2-inch squares. Place ½ teaspoon of filling on each square. Brush the edges with milk and fold the squares in half, point-to-point, to form a triangle. Wrap this lengthwise around your index finger and join the pointed ends, overlapping one over the other. Set to dry on a rack or floured surface and continue shaping the remaining cappelletti.

Allow them to dry for at least 15 minutes, then cook in salted boiling water to *al dente*, about 3 to 5 minutes, testing frequently. Drain and toss immediately with butter. Sprinkle a tablespoon of grated cheese over the pasta and serve, passing the grated cheese in a separate bowl.

Serves 6. Preparation time: 2¼ hours by hand; 1¼ with a pasta machine

PASTA ROLL WITH SWEET AND SOUR TOMATO SAUCE
Rotolo di Pasta con Salsa Agrodolce

Filling:

3 pounds spinach, or 3 10-ounce packages
   frozen spinach
2 tablespoons butter
¼ cup finely chopped onion
1 garlic clove, minced
1½ cups ricotta
1 cup freshly grated parmesan
1 egg, beaten
½ cup raisins
1 teaspoon salt
¼ teaspoon freshly ground pepper
½ teaspoon nutmeg

Sauce:

1 recipe Sweet and Sour Tomato Sauce (Page 47)

Pasta:

1 recipe Egg Pasta (Page 60)

Wash fresh spinach thoroughly, removing the stems and any bruised leaves. Place in a large, covered pot over medium-high heat. Steam in the water clinging to its leaves until just wilted, about 3 to 5 minutes, stirring once. Drain and rinse with cold water. To use frozen spinach, allow it to thaw.

Squeeze out the excess moisture in the spinach and chop finely. Melt the butter in a 10-inch skillet and sauté the onion over medium heat until golden, about 5 minutes. Add the garlic and the spinach, stirring to coat the leaves with butter; sauté for 5 minutes. Transfer to a mixing bowl and add the cheeses, the egg, and the raisins. Season with salt, pepper, and nutmeg, blend well and set aside.

Make or reheat the sauce and keep warm. Roll the pasta to ¹⁄₁₆-inch thickness and cut into 6 sheets 4-inches by 12-inches. Join the sheets in pairs to form three 8-inch by 12-inch rectangles. To seal the join, score along the longest edge of one sheet and moisten. Overlap with a second sheet by about ½-inch and press together. Repeat to form three large sheets of pasta. Place each sheet on a double layer of 12-inch by 12-inch cheesecloth. Divide the spinach filling into thirds and spread one portion on each sheet in a uniform layer that comes to within ½-inch of the edges. Starting at the shortest edge, roll the pasta in jelly-roll fashion, using the cheesecloth to help make a tight, even roll. Wrap the cheesecloth around each roll and tie the ends securely with string.

Bring salted water to a boil in a deep saucepan or roasting pan large enough to hold the rolls comfortably and deep enough so that they will be covered with water. Lower the rolls into the boiling water and reduce the heat so that it barely simmers. Poach the pasta rolls for 25 minutes, turning them once and adding water if necessary to keep them covered. Remove from the liquid and allow to drain. Unwrap the rolls from the cheesecloth and cut into ¾-inch slices. Spoon a bed of sauce on a heated platter and arrange the slices on top. Serve immediately.

Serves 6. Preparation time: 2 hours

AGNOLOTTI FILLED WITH SWISS CHARD
Agnolotti di Biete

Filling:

1 pound swiss chard

¼ cup butter

¼ cup finely chopped onion

1 cup ricotta

1 egg

⅔ cup freshly grated parmesan

1½ teaspoons salt

¼ teaspoon freshly ground pepper

½ teaspoon nutmeg

Pasta:

1 recipe Egg Pasta made with 2 teaspoons milk
  (Page 60)

2 teaspoons milk

Sauce:

1 recipe Béchamel (Page 51)

Remove the chard stalks from the leaves. Wash the leaves thoroughly and place them in a covered saucepan over medium-high heat. Steam them in the water clinging to their leaves until just wilted, about 3 to 5 minutes, stirring once. Drain, rinse with cold water, and squeeze the leaves dry with your hands or by pressing between two plates. With a sharp knife, chop finely.

Melt the butter in a large skillet and sauté the onion until golden and translucent, about 5 minutes. Add the chard and sauté for 5 minutes, stirring to coat the leaves with butter. Transfer to a mixing bowl and mix in the remaining ingredients for the filling; set aside.

Roll the pasta dough to ⅛-inch thickness and cut into rounds at least 2½-inches in diameter. Place a scant teaspoon of the filling on one half of each round. Brush the inside of the other half with milk and fold it over to form a crescent shape. Crimp the edges with the tines of a fork to be sure the agnolotti are tightly sealed. Allow them to dry on a rack for at least 15 minutes.

Make or reheat the sauce and keep hot. Cook the agnolotti in several quarts of salted boiling water, stirring frequently with a wooden spoon. They will take about 5 to 8 minutes, depending on the dryness of the pasta, so test frequently. Carefully drain and toss immediately with ½ cup of the sauce. Serve immediately, passing the remaining Béchamel sauce.

Serves 6. Preparation time: 2 hours by hand, 1 with pasta machine

SPINACH PASTA ROLL WITH THREE CHEESE FILLING
Rotolo Verde con Ripieno di Formaggio

Filling:

12 ounces mascarpone or cream cheese

¾ cup ricotta cheese

1 egg

½ cup freshly grated pecorino romano, or asiago

⅔ cup thinly sliced scallions, white and green parts

1 red bell pepper, seeded, in ¼-inch dice

½ teaspoon salt

¼ teaspoon freshly ground pepper

Pasta:

2 recipes Spinach Pasta (Page 68)

Sauce:

1 recipe Cold Tomato Sauce (Page 48)

Prepare the filling by mixing together all the ingredients; set aside. Roll the pasta to ⅛-inch thickness and cut into 6 sheets 4-inches by 12-inches. Proceed to form the pasta rolls following the directions for Pasta Rolls with Sweet and Sour Tomato Sauce.

When they have poached for 25 minutes, remove from the liquid and allow the rolls to cool to room temperature. Remove the cheesecloth, and cut into ¾-inch slices. Spoon the tomato sauce onto a serving platter and arrange the pasta on top. Serve at room temperature. *Serves 6. Preparation time: 2½ hours*

ASPARAGUS LASAGNE
Lasagne agli Asparagi

Filling:

4 pounds asparagus, or 4 10-ounce packages frozen
    asparagus spears
2 tablespoons butter
¼ cup finely chopped shallots
1 teaspoon salt
⅛ teaspoon freshly ground pepper

Sauce:

3 cups Béchamel (Page 51)
4 eggs
4 egg yolks

Pasta:

1 recipe Egg Pasta (Page 60) or 1 pound
    lasagne noodles

2 teaspoons butter

½ cup freshly grated parmesan

Peel the fresh asparagus; trim and discard the woody ends. Steam over salted boiling water or blanch in lots of salted boiling water until just tender, about 3 to 5 minutes. Refresh immediately in cold water and when cool, drain. Cut the spears 3-inches from the tips and reserve the tips. To use frozen asparagus, defrost the spears and cut them similarly. Chop the stalks in ¼-inch dice. Melt the butter in a small skillet and gently sauté the diced asparagus with the shallots for 15 minutes, or until the shallots are tender. Season with ½ teaspoon of salt and a pinch of pepper and reserve.

Roll the pasta to ¹⁄₁₆-inch thickness and cut into sheets 4-inches by 12-inches. Allow to dry for at least 15 minutes. Make or reheat the béchamel; when the sauce reaches a boil, remove from the heat and whisk in the eggs and egg yolks, one at a time. Do not reheat the sauce after adding the eggs. Mix 1½ cups of the sauce with the sautéed asparagus and set aside. In a separate bowl, mix ½ cup of sauce with the asparagus tips; season with salt and pepper and set aside.

Preheat the oven to 350°. Bring several quarts of water to a boil. Add salt and gently stir in the lasagne. Cook until the pasta is just *al dente*, stirring carefully every so often to prevent sticking. (Cooking time will vary depending on the dryness of the pasta, so test often.) Drain and rinse the lasagne in lots of cold water, taking care to prevent the sheets from sticking together, then pat dry with paper towels.

Grease baking pan about 9 by 13-inches with 2 teaspoons of butter. To assemble the lasagne, layer the bottom of the pan with noodles. Spread half the chopped asparagus mixture over this. Cover with more lasagne. Cover this layer with the asparagus tips, placing them lengthwise in rows and alternating ends so that a uniform layer of tips covers the surface. Cover these with another layer of noodles and spread on the remaining asparagus mixture. Top with a layer of noodles and spread 1 cup of the béchamel over all. Sprinkle with the grated parmesan and bake for 45 minutes. Remove from the oven and allow to settle for 10 minutes before serving.

Serves 6. Preparation time: 2½ hours with fresh pasta; 1½ with dried

GNOCCHI

Gnocchi may be made of all-purpose flour, semolina, ricotta, or potatoes. Though the Italians tend to rely on pasta and rice as their staples, the use of potatoes in dumplings is widespread. Potato gnocchi are particularly loved by the people of Verona where they are served with the simple sauce of sweet butter and freshly grated parmesan. The dumplings can also support heavier sauces as a pesto or Winter Tomato Sauce (Page 46). Potato gnocchi dough must be used as soon as it is made or it will get soggy and lose its shape.

POTATO GNOCCHI

Gnocchi:

4 pounds mealy baking potatoes

2 teaspoons salt

½ teaspoon freshly ground white pepper

⅛ teaspoon nutmeg

1½ cups flour

2 egg yolks

½ cup melted butter

½ cup freshly grated parmesan

Wash the potatoes and cook them in salted boiling water until just tender. Drain the water and return the potatoes to the pot over a medium heat and shake gently for 3 to 5 minutes to dry them. Allow them to cool slightly, then peel and mash them through a sieve or ricer to remove the lumps. (Do not use a food processor for this step.) Season with salt, pepper, and nutmeg, and stir in the flour. When the mixture is smooth, stir in the egg yolks with a wooden spoon, blending thoroughly into the gnocchi.

There are various ways to shape the dumplings. The easiest and quickest method is to pipe them through a pastry bag directly into the cooking water. Fit a large bag with a ¾-inch round pastry tube and fill the bag with gnocchi dough. Pipe a ¾ to 1-inch length of the dough and, using a small, sharp knife, cut it off at the end of the tube, letting it drop into several quarts of salted simmering water. Continue to form the gnocchi in this way, dipping the knife in the cooking water if the dough begins to stick to it. The gnocchi take only about 3 minutes to cook; when they rise to the surface, they are done. Remove them with a slotted spoon and allow to drain on paper towels while you shape and cook the rest. Toss the cooked gnocchi with melted butter and grated parmesan (or a sauce if you prefer) and serve hot.

A second way to form the dumplings is to roll the potato mixture on a lightly floured surface into ¾-inch rolls. Cut these into ¾-inch lengths. Allow the gnocchi to dry on the floured surface for 15 minutes, or shape and mark them according to the instructions in Parmesan Gnocchi on Page 89. Cook the gnocchi in batches to avoid overcrowding.

Serves 6. Preparation time: 1 to 1½ hours

SPINACH GNOCCHI WITH TOMATO SAUCE
Gnocchi Verde con Salsa di Pomodori

The egg whites in this recipe make a pleasingly light version of gnocchi, so light that they do not even sink in the cooking water. Using 2 spoons to form them helps to retain their shape, as does the brief baking just before serving.

Gnocchi:

1 pound fresh spinach, stems removed and thoroughly
   washed, or 1 10-ounce package frozen
6 tablespoons ricotta
2 tablespoons freshly grated pecorino romano
1 egg yolk
1 garlic clove, minced
½ teaspoon salt
⅛ teaspoon freshly ground pepper
A pinch of nutmeg
2 egg whites

1½ cups Summer or Winter Tomato Sauce (Page 46)
2 teaspoons butter

Steam fresh spinach in a covered pan over medium-high heat in the water clinging to its leaves for 3 to 5 minutes, until just wilted, stirring once. Drain and rinse with cold water. Allow frozen spinach to thaw. Squeeze the excess moisture from the spinach, then chop finely. In a mixing bowl, combine the spinach, the cheeses, egg yolk, garlic, salt, pepper, and nutmeg. Mix well and set aside.

Make or reheat the sauce and keep warm. Bring to a simmer several quarts of salted water; preheat the oven to 350°. In a clean bowl, beat the egg whites until stiff but not dry. Stir one-quarter of the whites into the spinach mixture, then gently fold in the remaining whites, retaining as much volume as possible. To shape the gnocchi, dip a teaspoon into the simmering water, then scoop out a rounded ¾ teaspoon of the spinach batter. With your other hand, dip the second spoon into the hot water and use its inverted bowl to shape the spinach mixture into a small, egg-shaped dumpling. With the second spoon, slip the dumpling from the spoon directly into the cooking water. Continue to form the gnocchi this way, but avoid overcrowding the pan. When each dumpling has cooked for 2 minutes, gently turn it over to cook for another 2 minutes. Remove to paper towels to drain.

Butter an oven-proof casserole and arrange the dumplings in it. Bake for 10 minutes in the preheated oven. Spoon a little sauce over the gnocchi and serve hot, passing the additional sauce.

Serves 6. Preparation time: 1 hour

 # PARMESAN GNOCCHI
Gnocchi alla Parmigiana

The method used for these cheese dumplings is the same as for *pâte à choux*, or cream puff pastry. Drying the paste increases the absorption of egg, making the dumplings lighter.

Gnocchi:
½ cup milk
½ cup water
½ cup butter, cut in ½-inch pieces
½ teaspoon salt
⅛ teaspoon freshly ground white pepper
⅛ teaspoon nutmeg
1½ cups flour
4 eggs
½ cup freshly grated parmesan

1½ cups Cheese Béchamel (Page 52)
1 pound fresh peas, shelled, or 1 10-ounce
     package frozen peas or 1 pound asparagus, cut
     into 1-inch pieces
Paprika, for garnish (optional)

Combine the milk, water, butter, salt, pepper, and nutmeg in a 1 or 2-quart saucepan. Bring to a boil over medium-high heat so that all the butter has melted by the time the water simmers. Remove from the heat and stir in all the flour, using a wooden spoon. When the mixture is smooth, return it to the heat and dry the paste, stirring constantly, until it begins to stick to the pan bottom. Remove from the heat and stir in the eggs, one at a time, beating them in quickly so that they do not cook. Beat the mixture well with the back of the wooden spoon to lighten the batter. Stir in the grated cheese. Bring several quarts of cooking water to a simmer and salt it. Make or reheat the cheese sauce and reserve; preheat the oven to 375°.

To form the gnocchi, refer to the recipe for Potato Gnocchi on Page 87 and shape as directed, or follow the method below. Roll the dough into ¾-inch rolls and cut into ¾-inch lengths. Hold one piece against your thumb. Using the back of a fork lightly dusted with flour, press the dough against your thumb and make indentations of the tines in the dumpling. The gnocchi will resemble a shell, with a hollow where your thumb has pushed in and ridges on the convex side. Form all the dumplings in this way, placing them as they are finished on a floured surface to dry for 10 minutes.

Cook the peas or asparagus in salted boiling water until just tender but still crisp. Drain and reserve. Cook the gnocchi in the simmering water in batches, to avoid overcrowding. Cook them just until they rise to the surface, about 3 minutes, then lift out with a slotted spoon and drain on paper towels. When all the gnocchi are cooked, toss them with the cheese béchamel and vegetables. Pour into an oven-proof baking dish and bake for 15 minutes. Garnish with paprika, if desired, and serve hot.

Serves 6. Preparation time: 1 hour

CHAPTER 6

CHEESE & EGGS

C heese and eggs are an alternative source of protein for the vegetarian, and the sheer range of Italian cheese and egg dishes means that they can offer a variety that is unlikely to become repetitive. It is a mark of the quality of their cheeses that in Italy they are given a course of their own, often with fresh fruit, served before dessert. Ricotta, a semi-sweet soft cheese, mozzarella, parmesan, and pecorino (the last two are generally reserved for grating only) figure throughout the recipes in this book, adding their very distinctive flavors and textures to dishes. The majority of this chapter, then, is given over to egg dishes and in particular, frittate, Italian omelets which can include anything from fresh vegetables to cheese or pasta as filling, and crespelle, or crêpes.

Of the cheese dishes, Piedmontese Fondue and Fried Mozzarella are probably the most widely known. The Italian version of fondue, unlike those served on the other side of the Alps in France and Switzerland, uses no alcohol and adds butter, milk, and eggs to produce a slightly richer, creamier consistency. The most distinctive feature, however, is the garnish of thinly sliced white truffle, a variety much prized by truffle-lovers and rarely found outside northern Italy.

Mozzarella in Carrozza ("buffalo cheese in a carriage") is known throughout the south, although it is originally a Neopolitan dish. To enjoy it at its best it should be eaten as hot as possible while the cheese is freshly melted.

91

PIEDMONTESE FONDUE
Fonduta Piemontese

Fonduta:
12 ounces Italian fontina, coarsely grated
1 cup milk
6 egg yolks
½ cup butter
⅛ teaspoon freshly ground white pepper
A pinch of nutmeg
White truffle (optional)

For dipping:
1 cup 1-inch cubes toasted Italian bread
2 cups blanched vegetables: asparagus, cauliflower
    and broccoli florets, beans, carrots

To prepare the fonduta, steep the cheese and milk in a covered bowl, refrigerated, overnight. Pour both into the top of a double boiler over hot, not boiling, water. Beat the egg yolks until frothy and add to the cheese mixture together with the butter, pepper, and nutmeg. Cook over low heat, stirring constantly, until the cheese is melted. Continue to cook, frequently stirring the mixture carefully so that it does not stick to the sides of the pan. As the yolks cook, the mixture will thicken; remove the pan from the heat immediately so that the eggs do not scramble. It is essential not to overcook the fonduta.

To serve, pour the fonduta into a heated bowl or individual bowls, garnish with thin slices of truffle, and surround with toasts and blanched vegetables.
Serves 6. Preparation time (not including steeping): 15 minutes

FRIED MOZZARELLA SANDWICHES
Mozzarella in Carrozza

1 recipe Italian Bread (Page 162), baked in a loaf pan
    and cut into ¼-inch slices, or 12 slices white bread
12 ounces mozzarella, thinly sliced

2 or 3 ripe tomatoes, preferably plum, thinly sliced
Salt to taste
Freshly ground pepper to taste
12 fresh basil leaves
4 eggs
½ cup milk
¼ cup clarified butter or vegetable oil

Place a layer of 6 slices of bread on your work surface. Using half the cheese, cover the bread with thin slices. Place tomato slices on top of the cheese and season with salt and pepper. Place a basil leaf on each side of the tomato on each sandwich. Cover with the remaining cheese slices and top each with another slice of bread, pressing down to make a compact sandwich.

Beat the eggs and milk together in a shallow pan and soak the sandwiches in this mixture for about 15 minutes, turning them occasionally until all the liquid has been absorbed. Preheat the oven to 350°. Heat the butter or oil in a large skillet over medium-high heat. When it is hot, sauté the sandwiches until each side is golden, turning once. (Depending on the size of your skillet, it may be necessary to work in batches.) Place the sandwiches on an ovenproof serving platter and bake for 10 minutes to melt the cheese. Serve immediately. *Serves 6. Preparation time: 45 minutes*

 # FONTINA AND TOMATO PIE
Tortino di Fontina

Italian fontina is made in the Val d'Aosta in northern Italy near the Swiss border. Its semi–hard texture and melting ability are similar to that of "Swiss" cheese, but its flavor is more pronounced, though not at all sharp. Fontina marries well with eggs and in this case, peppers, onions, and fresh tomatoes.

1 tablespoon butter
15 to 20 slices Italian bread, ½-inch thick
1 cup milk, approximately
2 tablespoons olive oil
½ cup thinly sliced onion
½ cup thinly sliced green bell pepper
½ pound Italian fontina, grated

¾ pound ripe tomatoes in ⅓-inch slices

Salt to taste

Freshly ground pepper to taste

1 tablespoon minced fresh oregano, or 1 teaspoon dried

4 eggs

½ cup grated parmesan

Preheat the oven to 400°. Butter a 9-inch pie or quiche pan. Brush the bread rounds with milk and allow them to soften slightly. Line the pie pan with them, forming a scalloped edge with the crusts and squeezing the bread close together on the bottom to fill all holes. Bake the crust for 15 to 20 minutes, until lightly golden.

Meanwhile, prepare the filling. Heat the oil in a skillet and sauté the onions and peppers until they begin to soften, about 3 minutes. Season with salt and pepper and reserve. When the crust is slightly brown, remove it from the oven. Cover with the onions and peppers; sprinkle the grated fontina and layer the tomatoes evenly on top. Sprinkle with the oregano and season with salt and pepper. Beat the eggs with the parmesan and a pinch of salt and pepper and pour over the filling. Bake for 20 to 30 minutes, until the eggs are set and the crusts golden brown. Serve hot.

Serves 6. Preparation time: 1 hour

FRITTATE

Unlike the French omelet which is quickly whisked over a high flame, frittate are cooked slowly over low heat. Of the different types of frittate, the open-faced style is probably the best known ... it is even eaten as a sandwich between two slices of crusty Italian bread. I've included several recipes for frittate, but this versatile dish can be made with most any vegetable or cheese, and the recipes can be adapted to accommodate those ingredients you have on hand.

Frittate are most easily made in well-seasoned metal skillets or non-stick pans. To season your skillet, pour in ¼ cup vegetable oil. Heat the oil until it is smoking, making sure all inside surfaces of the pan, including the sides, are coated. Remove the pan from the heat and pour off the oil. Add 1 tablespoon of fresh oil and ¼ cup salt, preferably the coarse variety. Using paper towels, scrub the oil and salt mixture thoroughly into the pan, going over every area several times. Discard the salt and wipe the pan clean with paper towels.

This pan should be used exclusively for frittate or crespelle and never washed: simply wipe the pan clean after each use with paper towels. If the pan is washed or begins to stick, repeat the seasoning process. (If only a small area is sticking, 'spot season' it by rubbing the warm pan with salt and oil, then wipe clean with paper towels.)

When preparing frittate, it is important to heat the oil in the pan before adding the eggs; then lower the heat so that the eggs cook slowly.

 # BAKED OMELET
Frittata al Forno

This frittata is not turned out onto a platter but served from the dish in which it is baked. Although the vegetables are arranged on the bottom of the pan, they rise to the top during baking. Ripe, red tomatoes can be substituted for the green ones, but they do not need to be sautéed.

1 small zucchini, well scrubbed, in ¼-inch slices

1 small eggplant, in ¼-inch slices

2 teaspoons salt

2 or 3 small green tomatoes, in ⅛-inch slices

¼ cup flour, approximately

½ cup olive oil

1 clove garlic, minced

½ teaspoon freshly ground pepper

8 eggs

2 teaspoons minced fresh oregano, or ½ teaspoon dried

2 tablespoons minced fresh basil

Salt the zucchini and eggplant and allow to drain, weighted with a plate, on paper towels for 30 minutes. Flour the tomatoes on both sides. Heat 2 tablespoons of olive oil in a large skillet and sauté the tomatoes over medium-high heat until lightly browned on both sides. Drain on paper towels and reserve. Wipe the salt from the zucchini and eggplant. In the same skillet, sauté the eggplant, in batches if necessary until lightly browned on both sides. Add more oil as necessary. Drain the eggplant on paper towels and reserve. Using the same skillet, sauté the zucchini over medium-high heat until lightly browned on both sides. Add the garlic to the pan and toss with the zucchini. Transfer to paper towels to drain.

Preheat the oven to 350°. Oil a shallow casserole 8 to 10-inches in diameter and arrange the vegetables in concentric circles on the bottom, alternating colors and textures. Sprinkle with pepper. Beat the eggs with the herbs and pour into the casserole. Bake in the preheated oven for 30 minutes, or until the eggs are set. Serve hot or at room temperature.

Serves 6. Preparation time: 1½ hours

ASPARAGUS OMELET
Frittata di Asparagi

½ pound fresh asparagus

6 tablespoons butter

8 eggs

¾ teaspoon salt

¼ teaspoon freshly ground pepper

2 tablespoons freshly grated parmesan

Peel the asparagus if necessary and slice ¼-inch thick on a diagonal, leaving the tips whole and discarding the tough, woody stems. The pieces should be about 1-inch long, in thin, flat ovals. Blanch in salted boiling water or steam over salted boiling water for 1 to 5 minutes, until tender but still firm to the bite. Refresh immediately in cold, running water. When cool, drain and reserve.

In a mixing bowl, beat the eggs with the salt and pepper. Heat ¼ cup butter in a 10-inch skillet and sauté the asparagus briefly over medium-high heat, just to coat with butter. Arrange the asparagus in a spoke pattern in the bottom of the skillet, and sprinkle with 1 tablespoon of cheese. Gently pour the eggs into the pan and cover. Reduce the heat to low and cook until the eggs are set, about 10 minutes.

If the eggs are not completely set on top but browned on the bottom, run a spatula under them and invert the frittata onto a plate. Add the remaining 2 tablespoons butter to the pan and when it is melted, slide the omelet back into the pan. Or finish cooking the omelet in the broiler, for 2 or 3 minutes until it is set.

Invert onto a plate, asparagus side up, and sprinkle with the remaining cheese. Cut the frittata into wedges and serve.
Serves 6. Preparation time: 30 minutes

 ## SPINACH OMELETS WITH TOMATO SAUCE
Frittatine alla Pommarola

These small frittate, a cross between omelet and crêpe, are made with an egg batter that is cooked flat quickly and rolled around a filling. Though I use spinach here, a filling of ricotta and herbs is also delicious.

2 pounds fresh spinach, thoroughly washed and stems
    removed, or 2 10-ounce packages frozen spinach
½ cup butter
2 tablespoons finely chopped shallots
¾ teaspoon salt
¼ teaspoon freshly ground pepper
⅛ teaspoon nutmeg
¼ cup freshly grated parmesan
2 cups Summer Tomato Sauce (Page 46)
3 tablespoons flour
6 eggs
¼ cup milk

Steam the spinach in a covered saucepan, in the water left clinging to its leaves, over medium-high heat for 3 to 5 minutes, stirring once, until just wilted. Or cook frozen spinach according to the package directions until just warm. Drain the spinach and rinse with cold water. Squeeze out the excess water with your hands or by pressing the spinach between two plates. Chop coarsely and reserve.

Melt ⅓ cup butter in skillet and sauté the shallots for 1 minute. Add the spinach, ½ teaspoon of salt, the pepper, nutmeg, and cheese, and set aside. Make or reheat the sauce. Sift the flour into a bowl and add the eggs; whisk together until well blended. Gradually add the milk and ¼ teaspoon salt; mix well.

Gently reheat the spinach mixture, stirring often. Melt 1 teaspoon butter in a 6-inch omelet, crêpe, or sauté pan over medium-high heat. When the butter is foaming but not brown, pour a generous ¼ cup of the egg batter into the pan and tilt the pan to coat the bottom evenly. Cook the frittatine until set and the bottom lightly browned. Put 3 tablespoons of the spinach filling in the middle of the omelet and roll both ends over it. Immediately invert onto a heated platter or individual plate. Continue to cook the frittatine until all six are made, adding more butter to the pan if necessary. Spoon a little of the heated sauce over each and serve at once, passing the remaining sauce separately. *Serves 6. Preparation time (not including sauce): 30 minutes*

 # PEA AND PEPPER OMELET
Frittata di Piselli e Peperoni

This style of frittata is actually a form of scrambled eggs. It is sometimes referred to as a *jambota* when two or more vegetables are used. Carrot, celery, fennel, or any other diced, cooked vegetable can be added to this dish.

1½ cups shelled fresh peas, or 1 10-ounce package
    frozen peas, thawed
1 large red bell pepper
3 tablespoons olive oil, preferably extra virgin
8 eggs
¾ teaspoon salt
¼ teaspoon freshly ground pepper
3 scallions, thinly sliced into rounds

Blanch the fresh peas in salted, boiling water until just tender. Refresh in cold water, drain, and reserve. Seed the pepper and cut into strips 1½-inch long and ⅛-inch wide. Heat the oil in a large skillet and sauté the peppers over medium heat for 3 minutes, until slightly softened. While the peppers are cooking, beat the eggs with the salt and pepper. Add the scallions to the peppers and toss with the hot oil. Pour the eggs into the skillet and stir in the peas. Continue to cook over medium heat, stirring constantly to break up the curds and keep the eggs soft. When the eggs are thick and custard-like, remove the pan from the heat (do not overcook). Spoon onto a heated platter and serve immediately.

Serves 6. Preparation time: 20 minutes

 # PASTA OMELET WITH TOMATO SAUCE
Frittata di Pasta con Salsa Pomodoro

This is an ideal way to use up leftover pasta already cooked to the *al dente* stage. The various pasta shapes and colors—from tiny stelline, or "little stars", to ziti (which makes quite a high omelet) and spinach fettucine—produce a wide range of interesting frittate.

3 cups cooked pasta, tossed with 1 teaspoon butter

2 cups Summer or Winter Tomato Sauce (Page 46)

8 eggs

1 teaspoon salt

¼ teaspoon freshly ground pepper

¼ cup minced fresh basil

2 tablespoons minced broadleaf parsley

¼ cup freshly grated parmesan

6 tablespoons butter

1 garlic clove, minced

Cook the pasta, drain, and toss with butter and allow to cool. Make or reheat the sauce. Beat the eggs with the salt, pepper, herbs, and half the cheese. Melt ¼ cup of butter in a 9 or 10-inch skillet over medium-high heat and stir in the pasta, coating it well. Stir in the garlic and sauté for 1 minute, stirring frequently. Pour in the eggs and smooth the top. Reduce heat to low; cover and cook for 10 minutes, until the eggs have set.

Run a spatula around the edges and underneath the frittata to prevent sticking. Invert onto a plate and melt the remaining butter in the pan. Slide the omelet back into the pan to cook the other side. (The omelet can be put under the broiler to set the top as well.) Sprinkle with the remaining cheese. Transfer to a heated platter and serve hot, passing the sauce separately.

Serves 6. Preparation time (not including sauce): 45 minutes

LETTUCE AND PEA SOUFFLÉ
Sformato di Lattuga e Piselli

For this lovely soufflé, I sometimes use a combination of escarole, curly endive, and romaine lettuce. Select whichever lettuce looks freshest in the market—except iceberg, which is too watery. Purée all the peas to give the soufflé a rich green color, or purée half and sprinkle the soufflé with the remaining peas before baking.

1 pound lettuce, thoroughly washed and cut
    in 1-inch pieces
2 tablespoons butter
1½ teaspoons salt
¼ teaspoon freshly ground pepper
⅛ teaspoon nutmeg
1 cup Onion Béchamel (Page 52)
3 eggs, separated
2 to 3 teaspoons butter
¼ cup fresh breadcrumbs
1½ cups shelled fresh peas, or 1 10-ounce
    package frozen peas
¼ cup freshly grated parmesan
1 egg white (optional)

Steam the lettuce in the water clinging to its leaves in a covered saucepan over medium-high heat for 3 to 5 minutes, stirring once, just until the leaves are wilted. Drain and refresh in cold water. When cool, squeeze out any excess moisture by hand or by pressing the lettuce between two plates. Melt 2 tablespoons of butter in a medium skillet and sauté the lettuce gently for 10 minutes, stirring to coat the leaves. Season with salt, pepper, and nutmeg; transfer to a bowl and reserve. Make or reheat the sauce. Remove from the heat and whisk in the egg yolks.

Preheat the oven to 425°, and set a rack in the middle. Butter a 6-cup soufflé dish and sprinkle with breadcrumbs. Blanch the fresh peas in salted boiling water for 3 to 5 minutes, until just tender, and drain, or thaw frozen peas. Add the peas to the sauce, reserving half to garnish the soufflé if desired. Add the lettuce to the sauce and purée in a blender, food processor, or food mill. (Be careful not to over purée, or the soufflé will lack texture.) Transfer to a mixing bowl and stir in the cheese.

Beat 3 or 4 egg whites in a bowl until stiff but not dry. Stir one-quarter of the whites into the soufflé base to lighten the mixture, then fold in the remaining whites. Turn the batter into the prepared mold and sprinkle the reserved peas over the top. Bake at 425° for 15 minutes, reduce heat to 350° and continue to bake for 20 to 30 minutes, until the soufflé has puffed and set. Serve immediately.
Serves 6. Preparation time: 1 hour

EGG AND PARMESAN FRITTERS IN TOMATO SAUCE
Pisci d'Ovu e Parmesan con Salsa Pomodori

Relatively inexpensive and simple to prepare, this hearty dish is always a good standby. Use your widest casserole or skillet (at least 10-inches in diameter) as the fritters will puff up in the sauce. In a smaller pan, the fritters should be made in two batches.

1 recipe Winter Tomato Sauce (Page 46)

12 eggs

¾ cup fresh breadcrumbs

1 teaspoon minced fresh oregano, or ¼ teaspoon dried

1 garlic clove, minced

¼ cup minced fresh basil plus ¼ cup minced broadleaf
    parsley, or ½ cup minced parsley

½ cup freshly grated parmesan

½ teaspoon salt

¼ teaspoon freshly ground pepper

3 to 4 cups hot cooked rice (optional)

Make or reheat the sauce in a wide casserole or skillet. Reduce the heat so that the sauce barely simmers. In a large bowl, beat the eggs until frothy and mix in all the remaining ingredients except the rice. Ladle this mixture, about 3 tablespoons at a time, into different parts of the simmering sauce, keeping each portion separate. Cover and cook for 10 minutes, until the fritters have puffed and are cooked through. Serve immediately, in the casserole or on a bed of hot rice.
Serves 6. Preparation time (not including sauce and rice): 30 minutes

CRÊPES
Crespelle

These delicately-flavored crêpes are every bit as versatile as their French counterpart. Fill them with fresh ingredients or leftovers—asparagus mixed with onion béchamel, zucchini or caponata in tomato sauce, scrambled eggs and peppers, and so on—and serve them as a main course or an appetizer.

When making crêpes, it is important to butter the pan properly. Too much butter will make them greasy and soggy; too little and the batter will stick to the pan. I've found this technique works very well: cut a small raw potato in half. Stick a fork in the rounded end and dip the potato in clarified butter or oil. Run the potato over the bottom of the pan to form a light coat of fat, repeating as necessary to keep the pan lubricated.

¾ cup flour

2 eggs

1 cup milk

⅛ teaspoon salt

1 teaspoon minced fresh herbs

2 tablespoons clarified butter or vegetable oil

Sift the flour into a bowl. Make a well in the center and break the eggs into it. Beat the eggs with a whisk, slowly incorporating the flour until all is absorbed and the mixture shreds from the sides of the bowl. Gradually add the milk while continuing to whisk. Season with salt and herbs, and allow the batter to rest for at least 20 minutes.

Cook the crespelle in a 6-inch crêpe or sauté pan. Premeasure 2 tablespoons of the batter into a measuring cup or ladle. Heat the skillet to a medium-high temperature, greasing the pan by the method above or by adding ½ teaspoon of butter or oil and tilting the pan to distribute evenly. When the butter or oil is hot but not smoking, pour 2 tablespoons of the batter into the pan, tipping it back and forth so that a thin, round, uniform layer covers the bottom. Cook the crêpe approximately 1 minute on each side, adjusting the heat to obtain an even, golden-brown color. Remove with a spatula, first side down (for easier rolling) and transfer to a plate, stacking the crêpes as they are finished. Add butter to keep a thin film of fat in the pan, as necessary.

Use immediately or allow to cool and wrap for future use. Separated by sheets of parchment or wax paper, they will keep a week refrigerated and up to 3 months frozen.
Makes 15 to 18 crespelle. Preparation time: 50 minutes

ZUCCHINI PANCAKES
Crespelle di Zucchini

These delicately-flavored savory pancakes are sprinkled with freshly grated cheese and served with a little butter, but you can fill and roll them with a mixture of ricotta and herbs. Or serve them with a sauce, such as Cheese Béchamel (Page 52) that has been thinned slightly with milk or water.

2¼ cups sifted flour

4 eggs

1 cup milk

1 teaspoon salt

¼ teaspoon freshly ground pepper

2 tablespoons olive oil

1 garlic clove, minced

1 teaspoon fresh minced oregano, or
    ¼ teaspoon dried

3 or 4 zucchini, well-scrubbed but unpeeled,
    coarsely grated

¼ cup vegetable oil

½ cup butter, at room temperature

1 cup freshly grated parmesan

Sift the flour into a bowl and make a well in the center. Break the eggs into the well and whisk them into the flour, just until blended. Gradually pour in the milk, whisking constantly, and season with the salt and pepper. Whisk in the oil, garlic, oregano, and zucchini. Allow the mixture to sit for at least 30 minutes to let the zucchini render its juices into the batter. The batter should be fairly thin so that the pancakes do not thicken as they cook. (You may want to test the consistency by cooking a small pancake and adding flour if necessary.)

Preheat the oven to 200°. Pour a small amount of oil into a heavy skillet or griddle and heat it to a medium-high temperature. Ladle 2 tablespoons of the batter into the pan and spread to a 3-inch diameter with the back of a spoon. Cook the pancake until golden brown on the first side, about 1½ minutes, then flip it with a spatula and brown the second side. Regulate the heat so that the pancakes cook evenly. Place the finished pancakes on a platter in the warm oven and continue to cook until all the batter is used. Pour in extra oil as needed to keep the pancakes from sticking.

Serve the pancakes hot, sprinkled with 2 tablespoons of the cheese and passing the remaining cheese and butter separately.
Serves 6. Preparation time: 1 hour

 # BROCCOLI CRÊPES
Crespelle di Broccoli

1 recipe Crêpes (Page 102)
4 cups broccoli florets
4 cups Cheese Béchamel (Page 52)
2 tablespoons snipped chives

Prepare the crêpes. Blanch the broccoli in a large pot of salted boiling water for 2 minutes. Refresh immediately in cold water and drain when cool. Reserve. Preheat the oven to 325°. Make or reheat the sauce over medium heat, whisking frequently. Pour 2 cups of the sauce into a large bowl and mix in all but 1 teaspoon of the chives. Add the broccoli and toss to coat well. Place a scant ¼ cup of the broccoli mixture in the center of each crêpe and roll the sides over it.

Arrange the filled crêpes seam-side down on an oven–proof platter. Bake, uncovered, for 20 minutes. Bring the remaining cheese sauce to a simmer; whisking frequently. Thin the sauce with a little milk or water so that it coats the back of a spoon. When the crêpes are done, spoon a little sauce over the center of the rolls and sprinkle with the rest of the chives. Pass the remaining sauce separately.
Serves 6. Preparation time: 1¼ hours

CHAPTER 7

RICE, BEANS & GRAINS

*I*taly produces most of Europe's rice crop and principally because of
the popularity of a single dish—risotto—it also consumes it. Like so
many of the most famous Italian contributions to cooking, risotto is
not one dish but many. More properly, risotto in fact refers to a
uniquely Italian method of preparing rice in which the rice is sautéed
then cooked slowly in a stock so that it absorbs the full flavor but each grain
still remains crunchy to the bite. (For this reason risotto generally should be
served immediately.)

Arborio rice from the northern Po River valley is preferred for risotto and
is available here through Italian and gourmet shops. It is a short grain rice
with starchy polish that contributes to the creamy consistency for which
risotto is celebrated. Although risotto is now made almost everywhere in
Italy, it is most commonly found near its northern birthplace. Its most classic
version is Risotto Milanese (which I have adapted to eliminate the meat but
retained the saffron which adds such a distinctive color and flavor).

Among the beans and grain dishes the most characteristically Italian is
Polenta. Polenta is made from cornmeal, preferably coarse-grained, mixed
with water and seasonings. It can be boiled, fried, baked, or grilled; served as
an appetizer, entrée, dessert, or even as a warming breakfast, rather like hot
oatmeal. For the beginner, the chief difficulty in making polenta is avoiding
lumps during cooking. The cornmeal should be added to the boiling water
in a slow, steady stream while stirring constantly with a wooden spoon to
prevent the mixture sticking to the pan.

RISOTTO

2 quarts White Stock (Page 32)
¼ cup vegetable oil
¼ cup butter
¼ cup finely chopped shallots
2 cups Arborio rice
1 teaspoon salt
⅛ teaspoon freshly ground pepper
½ cup freshly grated parmesan

Bring the stock to a boil, then reduce the heat so that it is kept just simmering. Heat the oil and 2 tablespoons of butter in a heavy 2-quart saucepan. Gently sauté the shallots for 3 minutes, until golden. Add the rice, stir to coat well and continue to sauté for 5 minutes, stirring constantly. Season with salt and pepper, then add ½ cup of hot stock, taking the pan from the heat as you stir it in. Return the pan to the heat, set at medium-low so that the liquid barely simmers, and stir constantly. As the stock is absorbed and the rice becomes dry enough to hold together in a mass, add another ½ cup of hot stock and continue to stir. Repeat until the rice is creamy in consistency but firm, *al dente* to the bite. This process takes about 30 minutes. Five minutes before the rice is done, stir in the cheese and remaining 2 tablespoons of butter. Serve hot.
Serves 6. Preparation time (not including stock): 40 minutes

 # RISOTTO IN THE STYLE OF MILAN
Risotto alla Milanese

Saffron is the distinctive ingredient in this dish, and its wonderful flavor and color are accented by fresh tomato. Saffron comes from the styles and stigmas of the crocus plant and must be harvested by hand, which is why it is so expensive. Fortunately, only small amounts are needed to have its aroma permeate a dish.

1 quart White Stock (Page 32)
¼ cup butter
½ cup chopped onion

1½ cups Arborio rice

1 pound plum tomatoes or 1 32-ounce can plum
  tomatoes, drained, peeled, seeded, and
  coarsely chopped

1½ teaspoons salt

½ teaspoon freshly ground pepper

¼ teaspoon saffron

¾ cup freshly grated parmesan

¼ cup finely chopped broadleaf parsley

Bring the stock to a boil, then reduce heat so that it is just simmering. Melt the butter in a heavy, 2-quart saucepan. Gently sauté the onion for 5 minutes, until golden and translucent. Add the rice and continue to sauté, stirring frequently, for 5 minutes, until the grains are opaque. Add ½ cup of hot stock and the tomatoes, and season with salt, pepper, and saffron.

Follow the basic Risotto method above for the technique of adding and stirring in the stock. The process will take about 30 minutes of constant stirring in all. When the creamy, *al dente* stage has almost been reached, stir in ¼ cup of cheese and the parsley. Turn the risotto into a heated serving dish and serve hot, passing the extra parmesan cheese.

Serves 6. Preparation time (not including stock): 45 minutes

 # RICE WITH SPRING VEGETABLES
Risotto Primavera

Make this risotto with any combination of vegetables, added according to their cooking times, or single out one vegetable that looks particularly good at the market. The very fresh look and taste make this risotto one of my favorites.

1 quart White Stock (Page 32), or water

¼ cup olive oil

½ cup chopped onion

½ cup chopped celery

1 garlic clove, minced

1 cup Arborio rice

1 teaspoon salt

¼ teaspoon freshly ground pepper

⅔ cup carrots, peeled, in 1½-inch by ¼-inch sticks

½ cup shelled fresh peas, or frozen peas

12 thin asparagus spears, or 1 10-ounce package
   frozen, cut in 1½-inch lengths

⅔ cup fresh sugar snap peas or fresh snow peas, ends
   removed and stringed, cut diagonally in half

¾ cup freshly grated parmesan

Bring the stock or water to a boil, then reduce heat so that it just simmers. Heat the oil in a heavy 3-quart saucepan and sauté the onion, celery, and garlic for 5 minutes, until golden and translucent. Add the rice and continue to cook, stirring frequently, until the grains are opaque and well coated with oil, about 5 minutes. Stir in the carrots and add ½ cup of hot stock or water, following the method for basic Risotto. Season the risotto with salt and pepper.

Continue to add liquid at 5 minute intervals for 15 to 20 minutes, until the rice has begun to soften on the outside but is still hard inside. At this point, about 5 minutes before the rice is done, add the fresh peas with a ladle of stock or water. With the next ladle, add the frozen peas (if used) and asparagus. Stir in the snap or snow peas just before serving, when the rice is creamy and the vegetables crisp; mix well. Stir in ¼ cup of cheese and turn onto a heated serving dish. Serve immediately, passing the extra cheese. Or serve the risotto at room temperature or chilled, tossing from time to time as it cools.

Serves 6. Preparation time (not including stock): 45 minutes

 # RISOTTO WITH WILD MUSHROOMS
Risotto ai Porcini

The rich, full flavor of dried mushrooms is brought out by soaking them in wine and using this liquid to cook the risotto. If they are available, fresh wild mushrooms, including the French *cèpes* or *morels*, are a delicious substitute for the *porcini*.

3 cups White Stock (Page 32)

1 cup dry white wine

1 ounce dried *porcini*

½ cup butter

¼ cup minced shallots

1½ cups Arborio rice

1½ teaspoon salt

½ teaspoon freshly ground pepper

½ cup freshly grated parmesan

Bring the stock to a boil, then lower the heat so that it is just simmering. In a separate pan, heat the wine to boiling and pour it over the dried mushrooms in a mixing bowl. Allow to soften for 5 minutes. If the mushrooms are sandy, wash them in the wine and lift them out of the liquid. Chop coarsely and reserve. Then strain the wine through a very fine strainer or paper coffee filter and set aside.

Melt the butter in a heavy 2-quart saucepan and gently sauté the shallots for 3 minutes, until they begin to soften. Add the chopped mushrooms and continue to sauté for 5 minutes. Add the rice and sauté another 5 minutes, stirring frequently so that the rice is well coated with butter. Add the mushroom liquid and stir constantly. When this has been absorbed, begin to add the stock in ½ cup measures, following the basic Risotto directions on Page 106. Season with salt and pepper. When the rice has reached the creamy, *al dente* stage, stir in the cheese and turn onto a heated serving dish. Serve immediately.

Serves 6. Preparation time (not including stock): 45 minutes

 # RICE CROQUETTES WITH MARSALA MUSHROOM SAUCE
Risotto al Salto con Salsa di Funghi alla Marsala

¼ cup butter

¼ cup chopped onion

1 cup Arborio rice

4 to 4½ cups hot water or White Stock (Page 32)

1 teaspoon salt

¼ teaspoon freshly ground pepper

2 tablespoons flour

4 eggs, separated

¾ cup freshly grated parmesan

¼ cup clarified butter or vegetable oil

1 recipe Marsala Mushroom Sauce (Page 58)

Melt the butter in a large saucepan and gently sauté the onion for 3 minutes, until it begins to soften. Add the rice and follow the directions for Risotto on Page 106, adding the water or stock, salt, and pepper.

When the rice is *al dente,* remove from the heat and allow to cool, stirring occasionally, for 15 minutes. Stir in the flour, egg yolks, and parmesan. In a separate bowl, beat the egg whites until stiff but not dry. Stir one-quarter of the whites into the rice to lighten the mixture, then fold in the remaining whites.

Preheat the oven to 350°. Over a medium-high burner, heat enough clarified butter or oil to cover the bottom of a heavy skillet. Ladle 2-inch risotto pancakes into the hot oil, but do not overcrowd. Cook until golden brown on the first side, 2 to 3 minutes, then turn gently and brown the second side. Remove to an oven-proof serving platter and continue to cook the remaining rice batter, adding more clarified butter as necessary.

Bake the pancakes for 10 minutes while you prepare the mushroom sauce. Spoon a little sauce over the pancakes and serve immediately, passing the additional sauce separately.

Serves 6. Preparation time (not including stock): 1¼ hours

 # PEA RISOTTO
Risotto di Piselli

As both peas and rice are very popular northern Italian foods, their combination in this dish is natural. The pea pods give a sweet aroma to the stock, which in turn is used to cook the rice.

6 cups White Stock (Page 32)

2 pounds fresh peas, shelled, and the pods

¼ cup butter

1½ cups Arborio rice

1½ teaspoons salt

½ teaspoon freshly ground pepper

½ cup freshly grated parmesan

2 tablespoons minced fresh parsley

2 tablespoons snipped chives

1 teaspoon minced fresh mint

Bring the stock to a boil and add the pea pods. Simmer for 15 minutes, then strain the stock and measure it, adding water to make 6 full cups. Return it to the pan and bring to a simmer. Melt the butter in a large saucepan and sauté the rice until the grains are opaque and well-coated with butter, about 5 minutes. Season with salt and pepper. Adding the stock one-third cup at a time, cook the rice according to the directions for Risotto on Page 106. When the rice is about 5 minutes from the *al dente* stage, add the peas with a ladle of stock. When the rice is creamy and *al dente*, stir in the cheese and fresh herbs. Serve immediately.

Serves 6. Preparation time (not including stock): 45 minutes

RICE WITH MOZZARELLA AND FRESH HERBS
Riso con Mozzarella e Condimenti

Mozzarella strands, warmed by the rice, give this dish a creamy texture, and freshly grated parmesan sharpens the flavor.

2 cups Arborio or long-grain rice

1 tablespoon salt

½ cup butter, at room temperature

½ teaspoon freshly ground pepper

¼ cup finely chopped fresh basil or broadleaf parsley

1 pound coarsely grated mozzarella

1 cup freshly grated parmesan

Bring 2 quarts of water to a boil and stir in the rice and salt. Boil for 15 to 18 minutes, stirring occasionally, until the rice is *al dente*. Drain and pour into a warm serving bowl. Toss with the butter, pepper, and basil or parsley. Add the mozzarella and continue to toss until the cheese has melted. Stir in the parmesan and serve hot.

Serves 6. Preparation time: 25 minutes

RICE WITH LEMON AND PARSLEY
Riso alla Limone

2 cups rice, Arborio or long grain
3 eggs
2 tablespoons lemon juice
1 teaspoon salt
¼ teaspoon freshly ground pepper
2 tablespoons butter
¼ cup minced broadleaf parsley

Bring a large pot of salted water to a boil. Stir in the rice and cook, stirring frequently, for about 10 minutes, until the rice is tender but still slightly crunchy. While the rice is cooking, beat the eggs with the lemon juice; season with salt and pepper. Drain the rice and return to the pan. Add the egg mixture, then the butter, stirring constantly until the eggs thicken and the butter melts. Stir in the parsley and transfer to a heated platter or bowl. Serve hot.
Serves 6. Preparation time: 20 minutes

 # WHITE BEANS WITH SAGE
Fagioli con Salvia

Fresh shell beans are tenderest when they are harvested in the early summer, and their cooking time then can be as short as 30 minutes. (As they dry the cooking time will increase.) Any fresh, dried, or canned variety may be substituted for the cannellini beans—lima, cranberry, red kidney, navy, chick peas, and lentils are all suitable. This aromatic dish is hearty and, with canned beans, quickly prepared.

2 pounds fresh cannellini beans, shelled, or 1 pound
    dried beans, soaked overnight, or 2 16-ounce cans
    white beans
2 teaspoons salt, for fresh or dried beans
¼ cup olive oil
1 clove garlic, minced

2 teaspoons minced fresh sage

½ teaspoon freshly ground white pepper

Simmer the fresh or dried beans in salted water to cover until tender: 45 minutes for fresh beans or 2 hours for dried. Boil the canned beans in their liquid. Whether fresh, dried, or canned, drain the beans and reserve the liquid.

Heat the oil in a 10-inch skillet and gently sauté the garlic for 1 minute, stirring constantly. Add the beans and continue to sauté for 5 minutes, coating the beans well with oil. Add ½ cup of the cooking liquid and cook the mixture to a creamy consistency (about 15 minutes) stirring often. Add more liquid if necessary. Stir in the sage and pepper and transfer to a heated serving dish. Serve hot.

Serves 6. Preparation time: 2¼ hours (with canned beans: 30 minutes)

LENTILS
Lenticchie

One of the oldest cultivated foods, lentils come in a variety of colors and textures. They also contain the most protein of any dried *légumes*, making them a good meat substitute.

¼ cup olive oil

½ cup chopped onion

½ cup chopped celery

½ cup chopped carrot

1 garlic clove, minced

1 pound plum tomatoes, or 1 32-ounce can plum
   tomatoes, drained (juice reserved), peeled, seeded,
   and coarsely chopped

½ pound lentils, soaked overnight

1 teaspoon salt

½ teaspoon freshly ground pepper

1 4-inch piece parmesan rind, or ¼ cup
   freshly grated parmesan

Heat the oil in a large saucepan and sauté the onion, celery, and carrot for 5 minutes, until they begin to soften. Add the garlic and continue to sauté for 3 minutes, until its aroma is released. Stir in the tomatoes,

lentils, salt, and pepper. Add water or juice from canned tomatoes just to cover. If using a parmesan rind, bury it in the lentil mixture (remove before serving). Simmer the lentils over low heat, stirring occasionally, for 1 hour or until they are tender and the mixture thick. Stir in the grated cheese and serve hot or at room temperature.
Serves 6. Preparation time: 1¼ hours

BEANS BAKED WITH TOMATOES AND LEEKS
Fagioli al Forno con Pomodori e Porri

¼ cup olive oil
½ cup chopped leek, white and tender green parts
2 garlic cloves, minced
2 pounds plum tomatoes, or 2 32-ounce cans
   plum tomatoes, drained, peeled, seeded, and
   coarsely chopped
1 pound dried white cannellini beans or Great Northern
   beans, soaked overnight
Salt and pepper to taste
1 4-inch piece parmesan rind, or ¼ cup
   freshly grated parmesan
¼ cup Pesto (Page 54), or ½ cup chopped
   fresh basil leaves
¼ cup freshly grated parmesan

Preheat the oven to 300°. Heat the oil in a 2-quart oven-proof casserole and gently sauté the leek for 3 minutes, stirring frequently. Add the garlic and continue to sauté until its aroma is released, about 3 minutes. Stir in the tomatoes, beans, salt, pepper, and parmesan rind, and bring to a simmer. Cover the casserole and bake for 2½ hours, stirring occasionally. After 30 minutes, uncover the beans and continue to bake, stirring often so that they do not stick to the bottom of the pot and burn.

    Fifteen minutes before serving, test the beans for tenderness. If they are nearly done, remove the rind, or stir in ¼ cup parmesan, and stir in the pesto or basil. Sprinkle ¼ cup of parmesan over the top and bake until the beans are tender. Serve hot.
Serves 6. Preparation time: 2¾ hours

KASHA SALAD WITH OLIVES AND RICOTTA SALATA
Insalata Saracena

Kasha is a cracked grain; when cooked, its high fiber content produces a good, chewy texture. In this recipe, kasha's nut flavor is set off with a classic combination of ripe tomatoes, ricotta salata, fresh basil, and black olives. Bulghur can be used equally well in this salad, which is remarkably quick and easy to prepare.

1 cup kasha or bulghur

2 cups water

1 teaspoon salt

¼ teaspoon freshly ground pepper

1 cup oil-cured Italian black olives, halved and pitted

1 cup grated ricotta salata

1 pound ripe tomatoes, preferably plum, peeled,
    seeded, and coarsely chopped

¼ cup Balsamic or red wine vinegar

½ cup olive oil

¼ cup minced fresh basil

2 tablespoons minced broadleaf parsley

Combine the grain, water, salt, and pepper in a covered saucepan. Bring to a boil and reduce the heat to low. Cook for about 15 minutes, until the grain has absorbed all the water. Transfer to a bowl and fluff with a fork. Allow the kasha to cool, fluffing occasionally to prevent sticking. When cool, toss the kasha with the remaining ingredients. This salad can be served at room temperature or slightly chilled.
Serves 6. Preparation time: 30 minutes

POLENTA

This is the basic method for making polenta. It is a hearty, comforting dish served hot and freshly made, with a pat or two of butter melting on it. For more elaborate polenta dishes, see Polenta Canapés (Page 29), and the following recipes for Polenta with Eggplant and Mozzarella, and Grilled Vegetable Polenta.

3½ cups water

1 teaspoon salt

¼ teaspoon freshly ground white pepper

1 cup coarse-grained cornmeal

Bring the water to a boil in a heavy saucepan and reduce the heat so that it simmers. Stir in the salt and pepper. Slowly add the cornmeal, letting it sift through your fingers in a thin stream while stirring constantly with a wooden spoon to prevent lumps. The water should be hot enough to bubble slightly but not so hot as to make the cornmeal boil hard and stick to the bottom of the pan. When all the cornmeal has been added, cook, stirring frequently, for 20 to 30 minutes, until the water is absorbed and the grains are tender. The polenta will wipe the sides of the pot as you stir.

Dampen a 12-inch by 18-inch cutting board or baking sheet. Turn the polenta onto it and spread to a smooth layer ¼-inch thick. Refrigerate until firm, at least 30 minutes. The polenta is now ready to be used in other recipes.

Yield: 2 cups. Preparation time (not including cooling): 40 minutes

POLENTA WITH EGGPLANT AND MOZZARELLA
Polenta con Melanzane e Mozzarella

The polenta in this dish is lightened with egg whites and layered with sautéed eggplant and tomato sauce, making it beautiful as well as delicious.

3 cups milk

1½ teaspoons salt

1 cup coarse-grained cornmeal

½ cup grated parmesan

½ cup olive oil, approximately

6 eggs separated

1 recipe Sweet and Sour Tomato Sauce (Page 47)

1 medium eggplant, in ½-inch dice

1 garlic clove, minced

½ teaspoon freshly ground pepper

8 ounces mozzarella, thinly sliced

Heat the milk to boiling in a heavy 2-quart saucepan and stir in 1 teaspoon salt. Reduce the heat so that the milk just simmers and add the cornmeal in a slow, steady stream, stirring constantly. Cook over medium heat following the directions for Polenta, above. When cooked, transfer to a large mixing bowl and stir in ¼ cup parmesan, 2 tablespoons oil, and the egg yolks, beating well. Reserve. Make or reheat the sauce.

Preheat the oven to 375°. Grease a 10-inch oven-proof casserole with olive oil. In a 10-inch skillet, heat the remaining oil and quickly sauté the eggplant over medium-high heat, stirring frequently and shaking the pan, until it is lightly browned, about 10 minutes. Add the garlic and season with ½ teaspoon salt and the pepper. Set aside.

In a clean bowl, beat the egg whites until stiff but not dry. Stir one-quarter of the whites into the polenta to lighten the mixture, then fold in the remaining whites. Spread half the polenta in the prepared casserole. Cover this with the eggplant mixture and spoon half the sauce over it. Lay all the sliced mozzarella over the sauce. Spread the remaining polenta over the cheese and cover with the remaining sauce. Sprinkle the parmesan over the top and bake for 45 minutes. Serve immediately.

Serves 6. Preparation time: 2 hours

 ## GRILLED VEGETABLE POLENTA
Polenta di Verdure alla Griglia

Make this dish with whatever vegetables are on hand. While it can be served as soon as the vegetables are stirred into the polenta, grilling it over an open fire or barbecue, or in a broiler, will produce a golden, crispy crust. For a quick lunch, make enough for leftovers, keep refrigerated, and pop them into your toaster oven.

½ cup chopped broccoli stalks, or chopped asparagus

½ cup diced potatoes

¼ cup olive oil

½ cup chopped onion

¼ cup chopped carrot

¼ cup chopped celery

1 recipe Polenta (Page 116)

2 teaspoons minced fresh dill, or ½ teaspoon dried

Cook the broccoli or asparagus in salted boiling water for 3 to 5 minutes, until just tender but still slightly crunchy; drain. Cook the potatoes in the same way, for about 10 minutes; drain. Heat the olive oil in a heavy skillet and sauté the onion, carrot, and celery until softened, about 10 minutes. Reserve the vegetables.

Prepare the polenta and when it is cooked, stir in all the vegetables and the dill. Moisten a cutting board or baking sheet and spread the polenta to a ½-inch thick layer. Allow to cool.

Cut the polenta into 2-inch by 3-inch rectangles and toast them over a hot grill or fire, or under the broiler, turning once, until each side is browned and crisp. Serve immediately.

Serves 6. Preparation time: 1 hour

PIZZA & TORTE

izzas need little introduction to an American audience. But the
flavor of a homemade pie so far surpasses the bland, rubbery
variety sold in stores and shops that they win over even the most
reticent eater of this Neopolitan dish. I have added cheese or
onions to my basic dough in some of these recipes and of course,
making your own ensures that you can use fresh ingredients in almost infinite
combinations.

The classic pizza is a crisp (not oily or spongy) crust baked to a golden
brown topped with sautéed fresh tomatoes and grated mozzarella and seasoned
with oregano and a little salt. To this you can add chopped garlic, freshly
grated parmesan or sliced olives. The best pizza is baked on a very hot brick
or stone surface, which gives the crust a crispness and flavor almost impossible
to produce in a modern oven. The closest equivalent of a stone oven is
achieved by baking on quarry tiles, available from building supply stores.
Before using them, wash and rinse the tiles and allow them to dry thoroughly.
Place them on the lowest rack in the oven and preheat to 500° so that the
tiles become very hot. Make the pizza on a lightly floured baking sheet (one
without a lip), then slide it directly onto the tiles. Adjust the heat to 400°
and bake, turning the pie if necessary to brown the crust evenly.

The savory torte can be served as quiche and are ideal for a light lunch or
buffet, while the Zucchini and Summer Squash Pie is a marvellously light
molded custard that could grace any meal.

PIZZA DOUGH
Pasta di Pizza

This dough serves as the base for most of the pizzas in this book and makes a 16-inch pizza with a ¼-inch crust and thicker edges. If the pizza is accompanied by another dish, this size is enough for 6 adults (or 2 teenagers!). To serve more, simply double the recipe: two pizzas are as easy to make as one. The dough, wrapped in plastic, can be refrigerated or frozen but do allow it to come to room temperature before using it.

4½ to 5 cups flour

2 packages active dry yeast

¾ cup warm water

½ cup olive oil, preferably extra virgin

2 teaspoons salt

Place half the flour in a mound on your work surface and make a well in the center. In a small bowl, sprinkle the yeast in ½ cup warm (105°–115°) water; allow it to sit until small bubbles appear on the surface. Pour the yeast and water into the well and mix the flour in gradually, taking from the sides of the well. Work all the flour into the dough. Knead the dough for 10 minutes on a lightly floured surface, pushing down and forward with the heel of your hand and folding back the dough with your fingers. Turn the dough a quarter turn each time you knead so that it is worked uniformly. The dough will be smooth and elastic. Lightly oil a bowl and put the dough in it, turning the dough so that it is covered with oil. Cover with a damp cloth and allow to rise in a warm (75° to 80°) place for 1½ hours, until doubled in bulk.

At the end of the first rising, punch the dough down. Turn it onto a lightly floured surface and knead in another 1½ cups of flour, ¼ cup warm water, the salt, and the olive oil (reserving some oil for the bowl and the pizza pan). Knead the dough for 10 minutes, adding flour as necessary to prevent sticking. Return to the oiled bowl and allow to rise for 1½ hours, until doubled in bulk. The dough is now ready for use or for freezing.

Preheat the oven to 400° and place a rack on the lowest oven setting. Grease a 16-inch pizza pan or baking sheet with olive oil. Punch the dough down and knead it for 1 minute to release any air bubbles. Lightly flour the work surface and roll the dough into a 16-inch circle. Stretch the dough in the center so that a ridge forms around the edges. This can be done with your hands instead of rolling it: Place the dough on top of your fingertips and extend your fingers to stretch it, or hold the dough with both hands and stretch it from the center outwards, rotating to work on a different section after each stretch. Place the dough on the oiled pan or baking sheet and cover with the topping you prefer. Bake for 25 to 30 minutes on the lowest rack in the oven, until the crust is golden brown, and serve immediately. *Serves 6. Preparation time: 3¹/₂ hours*

 # PIZZA IN THE STYLE OF APULIA
Pizza Pugliese

Apulia is a region in the sun-drenched south where tomatoes are especially abundant.

1 recipe Pizza Dough (Page 120)

Topping:
½ cup olive oil
1 garlic clove, minced
1 pound plum tomatoes or 1 32-ounce can
    plum tomatoes, drained, peeled, seeded, and
    coarsely chopped
2 teaspoons minced fresh oregano or ½ teaspoon dried
1 teaspoon salt
¼ teaspoon freshly ground pepper

Make the pizza dough according to the directions on Page 120. During the second rising, prepare the topping. In a large skillet, heat 2 tablespoons of oil and sauté the garlic briefly. Add the tomatoes, oregano, salt, and pepper, and sauté over high heat, stirring constantly, until the tomato juices have evaporated, about 10 minutes. Reserve.

Preheat the oven to 400°. Generously brush a 14-inch pizza pan or baking sheet with olive oil. Punch down the dough and knead for 1 minute to release any air bubbles. Roll or stretch the dough to a 14-inch circle and place it on the prepared pan. Make small wells in the dough, about 1-inch apart, by pressing down with your thumb. Drizzle the remaining oil over the pizza. Spoon the sautéed tomato mixture into the indentations and using the back of a spoon, gently press it in. Bake the pizza on the lowest rack in the oven for 45 minutes, until golden brown. Cut into wedges and serve immediately. *Serves 6. Preparation time: 4 hours*

PIZZA IN THE STYLE OF SYRACUSE
Pizza alla Siracusana

The influences of Greek cooking are prominent in this pizza, which features olives and eggplant as well as red peppers, tomatoes, and zucchini.

1 recipe Pizza Dough (Page 120)

Topping:
½ cup olive oil
1 small eggplant, unpeeled, in ½-inch dice
2 small zucchini, well scrubbed but unpeeled, in
    ½-inch dice
1 garlic clove, minced
Salt to taste
Freshly ground pepper to taste
¼ cup chopped red bell pepper
½ pound plum tomatoes or 1 16-ounce can
    plum tomatoes, drained, peeled, seeded, and
    coarsely chopped
8 ounces grated mozzarella
12 Sicilian green olives, pitted and chopped

Make the pizza dough and during its second rising prepare the topping. Heat 2 tablespoons of oil in a large skillet and sauté the eggplant over medium-high heat until lightly browned, about 5 minutes, adding extra oil as necessary. Add the zucchini and continue to sauté, stirring frequently, until it begins to soften, about 5 minutes. Stir in the garlic, season with salt and pepper, and transfer to a bowl. Using the same skillet, heat 2 tablespoons of oil and sauté the red pepper for 1 minute. Add the tomatoes and stirring constantly, cook over high heat until the liquid has evaporated, about 10 minutes. Season this mixture with salt and pepper and reserve.

Preheat the oven to 400°, and brush a 16-inch pizza pan or baking sheet with olive oil. Punch down the dough and knead for 1 minute to release any air bubbles. Roll or stretch the dough to a 16-inch circle, creating a lip around the edges. (If you prefer a thicker, chewier crust, shape the dough to a 14-inch circle.) Place the dough on the prepared pan and top with the grated mozzarella. Spread the eggplant mixture over the cheese, scatter the tomatoes over this and sprinkle the olives

on top. Bake on the lowest rack of the oven for 25 to 30 minutes, until the crust is golden. Slice into wedges and serve hot.
Serves 6. Preparation time: 4 hours

 # ONION PIZZA
Pizza di Cipolla

For those who love roasted garlic, this is the pizza to indulge your passion. Use the small cloves found at the center of the bulb, but don't peel them. When the pizza is cooked, squeeze the garlic cloves out of their skins to eat them. Cooking in the skins results in a milder though definite flavor. For the faint-hearted, the garlic can be omitted.

1 recipe Pizza Dough (Page 120)

Topping:
⅓ cup olive oil, preferably extra virgin
2 cups thinly sliced onions
1½ cups thinly sliced red onions
1 cup thinly sliced leeks, well rinsed
½ cup freshly grated pecorino romano
½ teaspoon salt
¼ teaspoon freshly ground pepper
12 small unpeeled garlic cloves (optional)

During the second rising of the dough, prepare the topping. Heat ¼ cup of the olive oil in a medium skillet and gently sauté the onions, stirring often, until they soften, about 5 minutes. Transfer them to a bowl and add the leeks to the pan. Gently sauté the leeks for 5 minutes, stirring frequently so that they do not color.

Preheat the oven to 400° and place a rack on the lowest setting. Generously brush a 16-inch pizza pan or baking sheet with olive oil. Punch the dough down and knead for 1 minute, then roll or stretch it to a 16-inch round. Place the dough on the pan and sprinkle with the cheese. Top with the onions and leeks and season with salt and pepper. Toss the garlic cloves with a little olive oil and sprinkle them over the pizza. Bake for 30 minutes, until the crust is golden brown. Cut into wedges and serve hot.
Serves 6. Preparation time: 4 hours

PIZZA IN THE STYLE OF VENICE
Pizza alla Veneziana

The crust of this pizza is made with asiago, a firm cheese with a sharp flavor. The fresh fennel in the topping blends wonderfully with the tomatoes to produce one of my favorite food combinations.

Dough:

4 to 5 cups flour

2 packages active dry yeast

½ cup warm (110°) water

2 eggs at room temperature, lightly beaten

⅔ cup grated asiago or pecorino romano

1 teaspoon olive oil

¼ teaspoon salt

Topping:

2 pounds plum tomatoes or 2 32-ounce cans
    plum tomatoes, drained, peeled, seeded, and
    coarsely chopped

1 garlic clove, minced

2 teaspoons salt

½ teaspoon freshly ground pepper

2 teaspoons minced fresh oregano or ½ teaspoon dried

¼ cup olive oil

¾ cup thinly sliced fennel

2 cups thinly sliced onions

½ cup pitted black olives, thinly sliced into rounds

Prepare the dough according to the method on Page 120. After the first rising, add the eggs, cheese, olive oil, and salt, along with the second 1½ cups of flour. During the second rising, make the topping. In a 10-inch skillet, cook the tomatoes with the garlic, salt, pepper, and oregano over high heat for 15 minutes, until the juices have almost evaporated. Transfer this mixture to a bowl and reserve. Heat 2 tablespoons of olive oil in a small skillet and gently sauté the fennel until it begins to soften, about 3 minutes. Reserve the fennel in a separate bowl. Heat the remaining oil in the same skillet and sauté the onion for 3 minutes. When it begins to soften, remove the onion from the pan and add to the fennel.

Preheat the oven to 400° and place a rack on the lowest setting. Generously brush a 16-inch pizza pan or baking sheet with olive oil. Punch down the dough and knead for 1 minute to release the air bubbles. Roll or stretch the dough to a 16-inch round; place this on the prepared pan. Spread the tomatoes evenly over the dough. Arrange the fennel and onion over the tomatoes, then add the olives. Bake the pizza in the preheated oven for 30 minutes, until the crust is golden. Cut into wedges and serve at once.

Serves 6. Preparation time: 4 hours

 # CHEESE PIZZA WITH EGGS
Pizza di Formaggio e Uovo

Eggs are a decorative and nutritious addition to this pizza. Be careful not to overcook this pizza; after adding the eggs, check frequently and remove from the oven as soon as the whites are set but the yolks still runny.

1 recipe Pizza Dough (Page 120)

Topping:

2 tablespoons olive oil

1 pound ripe tomatoes, preferably plum, peeled and
    sliced ¼-inch thick

1 teaspoon salt

¼ teaspoon freshly ground pepper

¼ cup grated parmesan

8 ounces mozzarella, coarsely grated

6 small or medium eggs

2 tablespoons minced fresh broadleaf parsley

Make the pizza dough and during its second rising, assemble the ingredients for the topping. Preheat the oven to 400° and brush a 16-inch pizza pan or baking sheet with the olive oil. Punch down the dough and knead for 1 minute to release the air bubbles, then roll or stretch it to a 16-inch round. Place the dough on the prepared pan.

Arrange the tomato slices over the dough and season with ½ teaspoon salt and ¼ teaspoon pepper. Sprinkle with the grated parmesan and bake, on the lowest rack in the oven, for 15 minutes. Remove the pizza from the oven and add the mozzarella, shaping the cheese to form six nests, each about 3-inches in diameter and ¾-inch deep. Gently break 1 egg into each well; sprinkle the eggs with the remaining ½ teaspoon of salt. Carefully return the pizza to the oven and bake until the eggs are set, about 8 minutes. Check often to prevent overcooking. When the pizza is done, sprinkle with parsley, cut into wedges, and serve at once.

Serves 6. Preparation time: 4 hours

 # THREE CHEESE PIZZA
Pizza Bianco

Dough:
1 recipe Pizza Dough (Page 120)
¼ cup chopped onion

Topping:
½ cup olive oil
½ cup thinly sliced onion
2 garlic cloves, minced
2 tablespoons chopped fresh rosemary
½ pound Italian fontina, coarsely grated
½ cup freshly grated provolone
½ cup freshly grated pecorino romano

Following the method on Page 120, make the pizza dough, adding the chopped onion in the well along with the yeast and water. During the second rising, prepare the other ingredients. Heat 2 tablespoons of oil in a small skillet and sauté the sliced onions until golden and translucent, about 5 minutes. Stir in the garlic and sauté another minute. Remove the onion and garlic and set aside. Heat the remaining oil in the skillet and sauté the rosemary for 5 minutes, until it sizzles and turns golden. Remove from the heat and reserve.

When the dough has risen for the second time, punch it down and knead for 1 minute to release any air bubbles. Preheat the oven to 400°. Brush a 16-inch pizza pan or baking sheet with the rosemary oil. Roll or stretch the dough to a 16-inch round. Place it on the prepared pan, pressing out toward the edges to form a lip. Brush the dough with rosemary oil. Spread the onion and garlic over the dough and top with the fontina; sprinkle the provolone and pecorino over this. Strain the remaining rosemary oil and drizzle it over the pizza. Bake for 25 to 30 minutes on the lowest rack in the oven, until the crust is golden and the cheese melted. Serve immediately, cut into wedges.

Serves 6. Preparation time: 4 hours

POTATO PIZZA WITH OREGANO
Pizza di Patate

The simple mashed potato crust of this pizza replaces the standard but time-consuming yeast dough. Use eastern baking or Idaho potatoes, and avoid new or red potatoes because they do not mash well.

Dough:

2 pounds mealy baking potatoes

2 tablespoons olive oil

1 teaspoon salt

¼ teaspoon freshly ground pepper

Topping:

⅓ cup olive oil

8 ounces mozzarella, grated

3 pounds ripe tomatoes, preferably plum, peeled, and
    sliced ⅓-inch thick

½ teaspoon salt

¼ teaspoon freshly ground pepper

1 tablespoon minced fresh oregano

1 cup grated parmesan

12 black olives, thinly sliced into rounds

2 tablespoons capers, rinsed and drained

Wash the potatoes and boil them in salted water until tender, about 40 minutes; drain. To dry the potatoes, return them to the pot over medium heat for 5 minutes, shaking the pan frequently. Allow the potatoes to cool slightly, then peel. Mash them with 2 tablespoons olive oil, the salt, and pepper, using a potato masher, ricer, or sieve.

Preheat the oven to 425°. Brush a 16-inch pizza pan with olive oil (reserving ¼ cup). Spread the mashed potatoes in an even layer, making a slight ridge around the edge. Sprinkle an even layer of mozzarella over the potatoes and top with the sliced tomatoes. Season with salt, pepper, and oregano. Sprinkle with the parmesan and top with olives and capers. Drizzle lightly with ¼ cup of olive oil and bake for 30 minutes, until the crust begins to brown at the edges. Serve hot, slicing as you would a pizza.

Serves 6. Preparation time: 1½ hours

CALZONE WITH TOMATOES AND MOZZARELLA
Calzone Napoletana

Calzone is a turnover made with pizza dough and any of the traditional pizza toppings. This recipe divides the dough and filling to make three turnovers, but you can easily divide it to make four or six, or even a dozen small ones to serve with cocktails.

1 recipe Pizza Dough (Page 120)

¼ cup olive oil

1 cup thinly sliced onions

1 garlic clove, minced

1 pound ripe tomatoes, preferably plum, or

    1 32-ounce can plum tomatoes, well-drained,

    peeled, seeded, and cut in 1-inch dice

1 teaspoon salt

¼ teaspoon freshly ground pepper

2 tablespoons minced fresh basil

8 ounces mozzarella in 1-inch dice

1 teaspoon olive oil

Make the pizza dough and during the second rising, prepare the filling. Heat the olive oil in a large skillet over medium-high heat. Sauté the onion, stirring occasionally, until lightly browned, about 10 minutes. Stir in the garlic and sauté briefly. Add the tomatoes and cook, stirring frequently, until the juices have evaporated, about 10 minutes. Season with salt, pepper, and basil and set aside.

Preheat the oven to 400° and adjust a rack to the lowest setting. Punch down the dough and knead for 1 minute to release any air bubbles. Divide the dough in thirds. Roll each portion to ¼-inch thickness, about 8-inches in diameter. Mix together the tomato sauce and cheese. Put one-third of the filling on half of each round. Brush the inside edges with water and fold the unfilled half of each circle over to form a crescent-shape. Press the edges together to seal.

Grease a baking sheet with olive oil and place the turnovers on it. Brush the tops with olive oil if a shiny crust is desired. Bake in the preheated oven for 10 minutes; then reduce the heat to 350° and continue to bake for 15 minutes, until golden brown. Serve immediately, cutting each in half.

Serves 6. Preparation time: 3½ hours

PUMPKIN AND SPINACH PIE
Torta di Zucca

1 teaspoon butter
1 recipe Short Pastry (Page 178)

Filling:
2 pounds fresh pumpkin, peeled, seeded, and
    finely chopped
Salt, to taste
1 pound fresh spinach, thoroughly washed, or
    1 10-ounce packed frozen spinach, thawed
2 tablespoons olive oil
½ cup chopped onion
5 eggs
½ cup heavy cream
½ cup freshly grated parmesan
2 teaspoons minced fresh marjoram,
    or ½ teaspoon dried
⅛ teaspoon nutmeg
½ teaspoon freshly ground pepper

Preheat the oven to 425°. Butter a 9-inch pie or quiche pan. Divide the pastry dough into two portions, one twice as large as the other.

On a lightly floured surface, or between sheets of parchment or wax paper, roll out the larger portion and line the bottom of the pan with it. Prick the dough with a fork and refrigerate. Roll out the smaller portion of dough to a diameter of slightly more than 10-inches; refrigerate.

Put the pumpkin in a colander, sprinkle with 2 teaspoons of salt, and allow to drain for about 10 minutes while you prepare the other ingredients. Place the spinach in the water clinging to its leaves in a covered saucepan over medium-high heat, stirring once, until it is just wilted. Drain and refresh with cold water. Squeeze out the excess moisture with your hands or by pressing between two plates. Chop the spinach coarsely. Heat the olive oil in a small skillet and sauté the onion until golden, about 5 minutes. Remove from the pan and reserve.

Break the eggs into a mixing bowl, beat slightly and reserve about ½ egg for the glaze. Add the heavy cream and beat until the mixture is light and frothy. Mix in the cheese, marjoram, and nutmeg. Squeeze the pumpkin dry and add it to the egg mixture, together with the spinach and onion. Season to taste with salt and pepper. Pour the pumpkin mixture into the pie shell and top with the remaining pastry. Crimp the top and bottom crusts together, cutting away the excess dough and shaping the edge decoratively. Glaze the pie by brushing with lightly-beaten egg and cut three or four steam vents in the top.

Use any leftover pastry to decorate the pie by shaping it into vines and leaves for the top. Bake the pie in the preheated oven for 15 minutes; reduce heat to 350° and continue to bake 30 minutes. Allow to cool on a rack for 5 minutes.

Serves 6. Preparation time (not including pastry): 1¼ hours

SPINACH PIE
Torta Verde

Pastry latticework makes this spinach pie an attractive luncheon dish (it can be cooked well in advance and reheated in a slow, 300° oven). The spinach filling is offset by the distinctive flavor of the gorgonzola crust. The spinach is cooked very briefly and refreshed in cold water to retain its green color and the texture of its leaves. Chop the leaves coarsely by hand or with the pulse setting on the food processor to avoid puréeing it.

1 teaspoon butter

1 recipe Gorgonzola Cracker dough (Page 169)

Filling:

2 pounds fresh spinach, or 2 10-ounce packages
  frozen spinach, thawed

8 ounces ricotta

3 eggs beaten

1 garlic clove, minced

½ cup freshly grated parmesan

1 teaspoon salt

¼ teaspoon freshly ground pepper

½ teaspoon nutmeg

Preheat the oven to 400° and set a rack in the lower third. Butter a 9 or 10-inch pie or quiche pan; set aside. Divide the gorgonzola dough in two pieces, one almost twice as large as the other. On a lightly floured surface, roll out the larger piece to a ¼-inch thickness and line the prepared pan with it. Roll out the remaining dough to a rectangle 10-inches by 8-inches and ¼-inch thick. (If you prefer, the dough can be rolled out between sheets of parchment or wax paper.) Reserve the pastry, refrigerated.

Wash the fresh spinach thoroughly in several changes of cold water. Cook the spinach in the water clinging to its leaves in a covered saucepan over medium–high heat, stirring once, until the leaves are just wilted. Drain immediately and rinse in cold water. When cool, squeeze the excess moisture from the spinach with your hands or by pressing between two plates. Chop coarsely. Place the spinach in a bowl and mix in the ricotta, beaten eggs, garlic, and grated parmesan. Season with salt, pepper, and nutmeg and stir to blend. Pour the mixture into the prepared pie crust and smooth the top with a spatula or knife. Cut the remaining dough into strips 10-inches long and ½-inch wide for the latticework. Place strips vertically, 1-inch apart, over the pie. Lay additional strips, 1-inch apart, diagonally across these, forming diamond shapes around the exposed spinach filling. Cut away any excess dough and seal the top and bottom crusts together, crimping the edges together decoratively.

Bake the pie in the lower third of the preheated oven for 10 minutes. Reduce the heat to 350° and continue to bake for 30 minutes, until the filling is set and firm to the touch. Cool for 10 minutes before serving, or serve at room temperature.

Serves 6. Preparation time (not including dough): 1¼ hours

EASTER PIE
Torta Pasqualina

The elaborate cuisine of Genoa is exemplified in this Easter Pie, which wraps the first spinach and artichokes of spring in delicate, flaky pastry. Easter Pie can be the centerpiece of your holiday table, but it is complicated so please read the directions through before beginning.

6 small artichokes, or 1 10-ounce package frozen
    artichoke hearts
Juice of 1 lemon for fresh artichokes
1 cup butter, approximately
½ cup finely chopped onion
2 teaspoons salt
½ teaspoon freshly ground pepper
1 pound fresh spinach, thoroughly washed, or
    1 10-ounce package frozen spinach
¼ teaspoon nutmeg
2 red bell peppers, prepared for Roast Peppers
    (Page 19), or 1 7-ounce jar roasted red peppers
½ pound phyllo pastry
1 pound ricotta
½ cup milk
7 medium eggs
2 tablespoons minced fresh marjoram
½ cup freshly grated pecorino romano

Peel away the outside leaves of fresh artichokes with a small, sharp knife. Remove the stems and cut off 1-inch from the tops. Trim away any green remaining on the leaves. Halve the artichokes and scoop out the chokes with a melon baller or spoon. Cut each half into quarters and toss with the lemon juice.

In a small skillet, melt 1 tablespoon of butter and sauté ¼ cup of the onion for 1 minute. Add the artichokes, fresh or frozen, and sauté, stirring frequently, until tender, about 15 minutes. Add more butter as necessary. Season with ½ teaspoon of salt and ¼ teaspoon of pepper and reserve.

In a covered saucepan, steam the fresh spinach in the water clinging to its leaves over medium-high heat just until the leaves are wilted, 3 to 5 minutes. Or cook frozen spinach just to heat through. Drain and rinse with cold water. Squeeze out the excess water by hand or by pressing between two plates. Chop the spinach.

In a medium skillet, melt 1 tablespoon of butter and sauté ¼ cup of onion until golden, 3 to 5 minutes. Add the spinach and sauté 5 minutes more, stirring to coat the spinach with butter. Season with ½ teaspoon of salt, ⅛ teaspoon of pepper, and a pinch of nutmeg; reserve. Cut the roast peppers into ¼-inch strips.

Preheat the oven to 400°. Melt ¼ cup of butter in a small saucepan. Brush a 9-inch pie pan with melted butter. To form the crust of the pie, lay a sheet of phyllo in the pan so that it overlaps on one side. Brush lightly with melted butter. Continue layering the phyllo, using eight sheets in all, brushing each layer with butter and placing the sheets at angles so that they will form a round top when folded in towards the center. When the sheets have been set in the pan, press them down with your fingers, molding the pastry to the shape of the pan. The crust is now ready to be filled with the vegetables.

Spoon the spinach in a mound at the center of the pie. Place the artichokes in a ring around the outer edge of the pan. Scatter the red pepper strips in a ring between the 2 green vegetables; set aside.

In a mixing bowl, combine the ricotta and the milk, ½ teaspoon of salt, ⅛ teaspoon of pepper, and a pinch of nutmeg; stir to blend well. Pour the ricotta into the space between the spinach and artichokes. Using a metal spatula or long knife, spread a thin layer of ricotta over all the vegetables.

With the back of a spoon, make 6 evenly-spaced wells in the ricotta in the area over the red pepper. Carefully break 1 egg into each well. Sprinkle with salt and pepper, marjoram, and grated pecorino romano.

Shape the top crust by folding the phyllo sheets toward the center, one by one, brushing each with melted butter. When all have been folded in, top with 2 flat sheets, centered and perpendicular to each other. Carefully tuck the ends in and under around the edge of the torta. To glaze the top, brush with beaten egg. Cut decorative steam vents in the crust in a sunburst pattern.

Bake the pie in the preheated oven until golden brown, about 1 hour. Remove from the oven and allow to set for 10 minutes. Cut into wedges and serve hot or at room temperature.

Serves 6. Preparation time: 2 hours

PEPPERY PIE
Torta Pepata

For this pie to live up to its name, you must be very generous with the pepper grinder. Taste the watercress mixture before baking the pie; perhaps you'll want to add even more pepper.

1 teaspoon butter
1 recipe Short Pastry (Page 178)

Filling:
1 large bunch watercress, leaves only
½ cup milk
4 eggs
2 cups heavy cream
1 teaspoon salt
2 generous teaspoons freshly ground pepper

Preheat the oven to 425° and place a rack in the middle. Butter a 9-inch pie or quiche pan. On a lightly floured surface, roll the dough to a ¼-inch thickness and place it in the pan. Prick the dough with a fork. To bake blind, or prebake the dough, line it with foil and fill with uncooked dried beans or rice. Bake in the preheated oven for 10 minutes. Remove the pan from the oven and carefully lift out the foil with the beans or rice. (The beans or rice can be re-used for baking blind; allow them to cool and store for future use.)

Chop the watercress by hand or in a blender or food processor. If you are working manually, put the chopped cress in a bowl, mix in the milk, and reserve. Or chop the cress in a blender or processor, then add the milk (with the machine running in the case of a processor) and mix well; pour into a bowl and reserve. In a separate bowl, beat the eggs with the cream, then add the watercress mixture. Season with salt and pepper, adjusting the amount of pepper to taste. Reduce the oven temperature to 350°. Pull the middle rack out slightly and set the crust on it. Carefully pour in the custard and gently push in the rack. Bake for 45 minutes, until the custard is set and slightly puffed. Serve hot.

Serves 6. Preparation time (not including pastry): 1½ hours

CHAPTER 9

VEGETABLES

T he Italian cook has an enviably wide range of good, fresh vegetables to work with that is almost second to none. Increasingly, however, markets in this country are selling a great variety of produce such as fennel and Swiss chard which until recently were rarely seen outside specialty stores.

As with salad ingredients, the best results are obtained when you use whatever is in season. There is rarely any substitute for vegetables straight from the garden, even if they are not as perfect or uniform as the specimens sold in the stores. But for the majority of us who do not have a large vegetable garden, we are dependent on the look and feel of the vegetables as an indication of freshness. In Chapter 1 I have given some pointers to follow when selecting fresh produce.

Mass production in agriculture has introduced a uniformity into our produce, often at the expense of flavor, texture, and variety. Cherry tomatoes and some pre-packed small mushrooms are examples of this; whenever possible I avoid using such vegetables and fruits in favor of fresher, locally grown produce. Sometimes this means being adaptable in my menu planning or spending a bit more time searching out the best, but I generally find it more than pays off.

In the recipes that follow I have used some of the techniques that Italians use, including braised, sautéed, gratineed, baked, and broiled vegetables. This is of course, by no means exhaustive and you should adapt these techniques to suit the vegetables you have on hand or add the sauces from Chapter 4 to prepare your own dishes. Good, fresh ingredients need little embellishment, and there is little better than a dish of fresh asparagus topped with sweet butter and freshly grated parmesan, or tender spinach sautéed with garlic and olive oil, or new potatoes and green beans in a pesto sauce.

VEGETABLES IN GORGONZOLA SAUCE
Verdura al Gorgonzola

This simple and elegant dish can be made with a variety of vegetables, including asparagus, green beans, celery or Swiss chard stalks, and zucchini.

1½ cups Gorgonzola Sauce (Page 53)
1 teaspoon butter
4 cups vegetable of your choice
Salt to taste

Make or reheat the sauce. Preheat the oven to 400°, and butter an oven-proof casserole. Wash the vegetables and cut them in 2-inch lengths. Blanch in salted boiling water for 3 to 5 minutes, until just beginning to soften. Drain the vegetables and arrange them in the casserole. Pour over the sauce and bake for 20 minutes.
Serves 6. Preparation time: 45 minutes

 # GREEN BEANS WITH MINT
Fagiolini Verde con Menta

2 garlic cloves, minced
2 teaspoons minced fresh mint
2 ripe plum tomatoes, peeled, seeded, and crushed
2 tablespoons olive oil, preferably extra virgin
2 pounds green beans
1 teaspoon salt
¼ teaspoon freshly ground pepper

Crush the garlic and mint in a mortar or finely chop them together. When you have a fine paste, add to the tomatoes, stir in the olive oil, and reserve. Trim the ends from the beans and cook in several quarts of salted boiling water, or steam over salted boiling water, for 3 to 5 minutes until just tender yet still firm. Drain the beans and toss them with the mint sauce. Season with salt and pepper and serve.
Serves 6. Preparation time: 25 minutes

GREEN BEANS WITH LEMON
Fagiolini Verde con Limone

Lemon and egg yolk make a light, delicate sauce for fresh green beans, but plan ahead when you want to serve this dish: it should be prepared at the last minute and served immediately.

2 pounds green beans
2 egg yolks
2 tablespoons lemon juice
¼ teaspoon freshly ground pepper

Wash the beans and remove their ends. Cook in several quarts of salted boiling water, or steam over boiling salted water, for 3 to 5 minutes. Test the beans frequently; they should be cooked until they have lost the raw taste but are still crisp.

While the beans cook, combine the yolks, lemon juice, and pepper in a large serving bowl. Mix these ingredients until they are well blended. Drain the beans (reserve ½ cup of the cooking water) and immediately toss them with the egg mixture. The heat of the beans will cook and thicken the yolks. If the mixture is too thick, add a small amount of the hot liquid and toss to distribute well. Serve immediately.
Serves 6. Preparation time: 15 minutes

SAUTÉED CAULIFLOWER
Cavolfiore Francese

1 head cauliflower, about 2½ pounds

1 tablespoon salt

6 tablespoons lemon juice

½ cup flour

3 eggs

½ teaspoon salt

¼ teaspoon freshly ground white pepper

⅓ cup vegetable oil, approximately

½ cup butter

¼ cup finely chopped broadleaf parsley (optional)

Trim the cauliflower and cut it into florets of equal size. In a large pot bring water to a boil and stir in the salt and 2 tablespoons of lemon juice. Add the cauliflower and cook for 5 minutes, until just tender when pierced with a sharp knife. Drain the cauliflower and immediately refresh in cold water. When the florets are cool, drain them.

Preheat the oven to 350°. Lightly beat the eggs with the salt and pepper. Flour several florets and dip them in the eggs, turning to coat completely. Heat 2 tablespoons of oil in a large skillet over medium-high heat and when the oil is hot, add a layer of cauliflower without overcrowding the pan. Sauté the cauliflower until lightly browned on all sides. As they are done, remove with a slotted spoon and drain on paper towels. Continue to coat and sauté the cauliflower in batches, adding more oil to the pan as necessary. Transfer the sautéed florets to an oven-proof platter and reserve in the preheated oven while you make the sauce.

Pour the remaining ¼ cup of lemon juice into the same skillet and bring to a boil, stirring with a wooden spoon to scrape up the brown bits. Cut the butter in several pieces, reduce the heat to low and swirl in the butter with a whisk. When the butter has melted, pour the lemon sauce over the cauliflower and toss with the parsley if desired. *Serves 6. Preparation time: 30 minutes*

FENNEL GRATIN
Finocchio al Formaggio

The tender inside layers of the fennel bulb have the most delicate flavor, but the outside layers and stalks can be used in stock or soup. Save sprigs of fennel leaves to garnish the baked gratin.

2 cups Cheese Béchamel (Page 52)
1 teaspoon butter
4 large heads fennel
1 teaspoon salt
½ teaspoon freshly ground white pepper

Make the sauce, saving the cheeses to add just before pouring over the fennel. Preheat the oven to 400° and butter an oven-proof casserole. Trim the root end of the fennel bulbs and cut off the stalks. Peel away the outer layers. Slice each bulb in half and remove the core. Cut the bulbs into thin slices. Blanch the fennel in boiling water for 1 minute, drain, and rinse with cold water. Add the fontina to the sauce and stir in the fennel. Pour this mixture into the casserole, and sprinkle the grated parmesan, salt, and pepper over the top. Bake for 20 minutes, until the cheese is lightly browned. Garnish with fennel sprigs.
Serves 6. Preparation time: 45 minutes

 ## BRAISED LEEKS
Porri in Umido

The proportions below are for leeks about ¾-inch in diameter. If you have smaller leeks, do not cut them in half but slit the green part to make cleaning easier. If the leeks are larger, quarter them, cutting off as little of the root end as possible to keep them intact. Whole braised leeks are attractive arranged around any main course, or served as a hot or cold appetizer.

12 medium leeks
½ cup olive oil
2 garlic cloves, minced
1 pound plum tomatoes or 1 32-ounce can
    plum tomatoes, drained, peeled, seeded, and
    coarsely chopped

1½ teaspoons salt

½ teaspoon freshly ground pepper

2 tablespoons lemon juice

¼ cup capers, rinsed and drained

2 tablespoons minced broadleaf parsley

Cut off the root ends of the leeks. Remove all but 2-inches of the green leaves and slit through the tops if necessary to clean. Wash the leeks well in cold water, peeling and discarding any outside layers that are bruised. Halve the leeks lengthwise. Bring a large pot of salted water to a boil and blanch the leeks for 3 minutes. Refresh in cold water and drain.

Heat the oil in a large skillet and sauté the garlic until golden and fragrant, about 2 minutes. Add the leeks and toss with the hot oil. Stir in the chopped tomatoes and season with salt and pepper. Cover the skillet and simmer over low heat for 10 minutes until the leeks are just tender, turning them over halfway through the cooking process. Add water if necessary and shake the pan occasionally to keep the leeks from sticking to the bottom. Arrange the leeks on a heated platter, sprinkle with the lemon juice, capers, and parsley, and serve hot. Or allow them to cool and refrigerate, then sprinkle with the lemon juice, capers, and parsley just before serving.

Serves 6. Preparation time: 25 minutes

 # ROASTED MUSHROOMS
Funghi Arrosti

This is a savory mixture of mushrooms, potatoes, and cheese, oven-roasted in hot olive oil to a golden crispness. In the late summer and fall, when wild mushrooms are abundant in the countryside, this is a popular dish in Italian restaurants and homes. Fresh *porcini* or French *chanterelles* can be used, but fresh wild mushrooms are not always available and are quite costly so I've substituted regular mushrooms in the recipe below.

1½ pounds white, tightly closed mushrooms

2 pounds new or red potatoes

½ cup olive oil

½ cup grated parmesan or pecorino romano

1 garlic clove, minced

1 teaspoon salt

½ teaspoon freshly ground white pepper

¼ cup finely chopped broadleaf parsley

Preheat the oven to 450°. Wipe the mushrooms with a damp cloth. Cut off and quarter the stems, leaving the caps whole. Peel the potatoes and slice them ¼-inch thick. Pour the oil into a roasting pan and heat it in the oven until almost smoking, about 5 minutes. Toss the potatoes in the hot oil and roast them for 5 minutes. Stir the potatoes and reduce the heat to 375°. Continue to roast for 15 minutes, then remove from the oven to add the other ingredients. Add the mushrooms to the pan, together with the cheese, garlic, salt, pepper, and 2 tablespoons of the parsley. Toss everything together to coat well with hot oil. Return the pan to the oven for 10 minutes, until the potatoes and mushrooms are golden. Transfer to a heated platter and sprinkle with the remaining parsley.
Serves 6. Preparation time: 45 minutes

 # PEPERONATA

Peperonata uses unpeeled sweet peppers—green, red, yellow, even the more exotic purple bell pepper. A colorful opener to any meal, it can be served too as a hot or cold vegetable or as a relish.

8 large bell peppers, any combination of colors

¼ cup olive oil, preferably extra virgin

2 cups thinly sliced onion

1 garlic clove, minced

1 bay leaf

1 pound plum tomatoes, peeled, seeded, and chopped

¾ teaspoon salt

⅛ teaspoon freshly ground pepper

¼ cup red wine vinegar

1 tablespoon minced fresh basil

Halve the peppers, core them, and remove any white pith in their cavities. Cut them lengthwise in ½-inch strips. Heat the oil in a large skillet and gently sauté the onions until golden and translucent, about 5 minutes. Add the garlic and bay leaf, and continue to sauté for 3

minutes. Add the peppers and sauté over medium heat for 5 minutes, stirring frequently. Stir in the tomatoes and season with salt and pepper. Cook the vegetables until the juice from the tomatoes has evaporated, about 15 minutes. Remove the bay leaf and stir in the vinegar and the basil. Marinate the peperonata at room temperature for at least 30 minutes, and serve reheated or at room temperature.
Serves 6. Preparation time: 40 minutes

PEPPERS IN THE STYLE OF SARDINIA
Peperoni Sardi

6 yellow bell peppers

1 teaspoon minced chili pepper, or ½ teaspoon red
    pepper flakes

½ cup raisins

1 garlic clove, minced

1 cup cherry tomatoes, halved

2 tablespoons olive oil, preferably extra virgin

Roast the peppers using the method on Page 19. Peel and cut them into ¼-inch strips. Toss the peppers with the remaining ingredients and marinate for at least 30 minutes, tossing occasionally. The peppers can be served hot or cold, and will keep in the refrigerator for several days; return to room temperature before serving.
Serves 6. Preparation time (not including marinating): 35 minutes

POTATO GRATIN
Patate al Formaggio

Combining potatoes and dairy products forms a whole protein, and this dish adds tomatoes for flavor and color. The oregano and plenty of freshly ground pepper give it a spiciness common in the dishes of southern Italy. Though the gratins so popular in France are rare in Italian cooking, I do think this is a distant if 'poor' relative.

½ cup olive oil, approximately

2 pounds new or red potatoes, peeled and sliced
    ½-inch thick

2 teaspoons salt

1 teaspoon freshly ground pepper

⅔ cup freshly grated pecorino romano

2 onions, sliced ½-inch thick

2 pounds ripe tomatoes, peeled if desired, sliced
    ½-inch thick

½ cup fresh breadcrumbs, preferably from
    Italian bread

1 tablespoon minced fresh oregano, or
    1 teaspoon dried

Preheat the oven to 400°. Brush an oven-proof casserole with olive oil. Place a layer of potatoes on the bottom; sprinkle them with salt, pepper, olive oil, and cheese. Cover with a layer of onion rings, and arrange tomato slices over the onions. Season the tomatoes with salt and pepper and sprinkle with a little cheese. Continue to layer potatoes, onions, and tomatoes, sprinkling salt, pepper, oil, and cheese on each layer of potatoes. When all the vegetables are used, sprinkle the casserole with a mixture of breadcrumbs and oregano. Drizzle olive oil over the top and bake until the potatoes are tender, about 45 minutes.

Serves 6. Preparation time: 1¼ hours

 # SPINACH WITH RAISINS AND PINE NUTS
Spinaci alla Genovese

3 pounds fresh spinach, stems removed and thoroughly
    washed, or 3 10-ounce packages frozen spinach

2 tablespoons butter

2 tablespoons olive oil

1 garlic clove, minced

½ cup raisins, plumped in 1 cup hot water for
    15 minutes

1 ½ teaspoons salt

½ teaspoon freshly ground pepper

½ cup lightly toasted pine nuts

Cook fresh spinach in the water clinging to its leaves in a covered saucepan over medium-high heat for 3 to 5 minutes, until just wilted, stirring once. If you are using frozen spinach, cook it according to the package directions until it is just thawed. Drain the spinach and cool slightly. Squeeze out the excess moisture with your hands or by pressing between two plates, then chop coarsely.

Heat the butter and oil in a medium skillet and lightly sauté the garlic. Add the spinach and drained raisins, stir to coat well, and cook over medium-high heat for 5 minutes, stirring often. Season with salt and pepper, stir in the nuts, and serve.
Serves 6. Preparation time: 25 minutes

SWISS CHARD AND MUSHROOM PÂTÉ
Sformato di Bietole e Funghi

This attractive pâté is lined with Swiss chard leaves and topped with thin slices of lemon and a fan of sliced mushrooms. Serve it hot or at room temperature, as a first course or light lunch dish.

2 pounds Swiss chard leaves, removed from stems and
    thoroughly washed

¼ cup butter, plus 1 teaspoon

1 pound fresh mushrooms

2 garlic cloves, minced

2 tablespoons lemon juice

2 teaspoons salt

¼ teaspoon freshly ground pepper

½ teaspoon Tabasco sauce, or to taste

5 eggs

½ cup freshly grated asiago or parmesan

1 lemon, thinly sliced into rounds

When removing the chard leaves from their stems and washing them, keep some of the larger leaves intact to line the mold. Steam the leaves in the water clinging to them in a covered saucepan over high heat for 5 minutes, stirring once, until just wilted. Drain and rinse with cold water, then pat dry. Butter a loaf pan and line it with a layer of leaves. Squeeze the excess moisture from the remaining leaves, either by hand or pressing between two plates; chop coarsely and set aside. Wipe the mushrooms with a damp cloth and trim the stems. Choose one attractive mushroom and reserve for garnish. Chop the mushrooms in ¼-inch dice and toss with lemon juice to prevent discoloring. Melt the ¼ cup of butter in a large skillet and sauté the mushrooms until lightly browned. Add the garlic and sauté for 2 minutes, stirring frequently. Add the chard and sauté 5 minutes, stirring to coat the leaves well. Season with salt, pepper, and Tabasco. Transfer the vegetables to a bowl and allow to cool slightly.

Preheat the oven to 350°. Lightly beat the eggs in a mixing bowl and stir in the cheese. Beat in the mushroom mixture and pour it into the prepared pan. Bake the mold for 30 minutes, until the eggs have set. Remove from the oven and allow the mold to sit for 5 minutes. Carefully run a knife around the edges of the pan to loosen the pâté. To unmold, place the serving platter on top and invert; remove the loaf pan.

Cut the reserved mushroom in thin slices and toss with lemon juice. Arrange the slices in a fan shape at the center of the pâté, then add the lemon slices.

Serves 6. Preparation time: 1 hour

 # SAUTÉED TOMATOES
Pomodori Saltati

Ripe tomatoes are best for this quick sauté. Cooking the chunks of tomato over high heat softens the outsides while the insides remain juicy and fresh.

½ cup olive oil, preferably extra virgin
2 cups day-old bread cubes (½-inch), preferably
    from Italian bread
2 garlic cloves, minced
2 pounds ripe plum tomatoes or 2 32-ounce cans plum
    tomatoes, drained, peeled, seeded, in 1-inch dice

½ cup tightly packed fresh basil leaves,
  coarsely chopped

1 teaspoon salt

¼ teaspoon freshly ground pepper

¼ cup Balsamic or red wine vinegar

Heat the olive oil in a large skillet and sauté the bread cubes quickly over medium-high heat so that they brown on all sides. Remove the croutons with a slotted spoon and drain on paper towels. Add the garlic to the pan, then stir in the tomatoes. Turn the heat to high and sauté, stirring constantly, until most of the juice has evaporated, about 2 or 3 minutes. Stir in the basil, salt, pepper, and vinegar. Toss with the croutons and serve at once.

Serves 6. Preparation time: 15 minutes

ZUCCHINI WITH PARMESAN
Zucchini alla Parmigiana

This is a very quick and easy dish to prepare. In fact, any vegetable coarsely chopped or grated can be prepared this way. Some, such as artichokes and green beans, need parboiling but others, such as spinach and the zucchini used here, can be sautéed raw. Salting the zucchini helps to draw out its water and keeps it from absorbing too much oil.

3 or 4 medium zucchini, well-scrubbed but
  unpeeled, coarsely grated

2 teaspoons salt

2 tablespoons butter

½ teaspoon freshly ground pepper.

½ cup freshly grated parmesan

Salt the grated zucchini and place it in a colander in the sink. Allow the zucchini to drain for 5 minutes, then squeeze out the excess moisture. Heat the butter in a large skillet and sauté the zucchini over medium-high heat for 2 to 3 minutes, until just turning translucent. Season with pepper, toss with the cheese, and serve.

Serves 6. Preparation time: 15 minutes

CHAPTER 10

SALADS

*T*raditionally Italians serve the salad as a separate course at the end of a meal, before dessert or cheese. The function is as much to refresh the palate as to form a break between two distinct parts of a meal. Salads, then, are intended more to provide a change in texture and taste (even pace) than to satisfy an appetite; and for this reason the simple green salad, in all its infinite variations, has become the most popular.

The key to a successful salad is using only the freshest ingredients in season—the crispest lettuce or spinach, the ripest tomatoes, the most tender asparagus. With so many fruits and vegetables now available in the markets all year round, it is easy to forget that they do have seasons. But a salad will quickly reveal the deficiency of produce and in winter months I always try to select from the wide variety of seasonal vegetables—carrots, Jerusalem artichokes, spinach, fennel, and cabbage. There is nothing worse than a Mozzarella and Tomato Salad made with the bland, watery tomatoes that appear in the stores during winter months.

To compose a green salad, begin with one vegetable as a base and build flavors and textures around that. Romaine, escarole, and Bibb are good to start with, being crisp and flavorful without any bitterness. Boston and leaf lettuce are soft-leafed and tend to be perishable unless handled with care. Their delicate taste and texture underline the flavors of any salad or cold antipasto. Curly endive, dandelion, and red lettuce (radicchio) add texture and color to a salad with their curls and splashes of magenta and green, and are hardier greens which keep well in the crisper. Italian salads are simple, with one ingredient never overwhelming another, but rather forming a balance of flavors and textures. Because of their distinctive flavors, radicchio, escarole, Belgian endive, and arugula should be used with discretion to act as highlights in the salad. Equally, fresh herbs should be treated with a light hand.

The Italians also serve salata mista, or mixed salad, composed of several vegetables, often precooked, combined with each other or with fresh greens and lightly dressed. Artichokes, green beans, asparagus, broccoli, cauliflower, and peas may be added as blanched vegetables. Raw vegetables such as mushrooms, radishes, peppers, grated carrots, and Jerusalem artichokes add texture to a green salad and can be cut into shapes as a garnish.

The dressing is the essential part of a salad. For most, an oil to vinegar ratio of 3 to 1 is suitable, with a little salt and pepper; minced fresh herbs or a clove of garlic can be added to taste. Astringent fruits or vegetables such as oranges, radicchio, or Belgian endive can mean that the proportion of oil should be increased, depending on the other ingredients of the salad. Similarly, potatoes, broccoli, carrots, and other crisper vegetables need less oil. When assembling your own salad, the secret is to mix and taste the dressing until you feel you have the right balance. Only the most practiced hand can pour the oil, vinegar, and seasonings directly onto the salad.

Salad oil should always be olive oil, and for me there is no substitute for the best extra virgin oil. This should be married with a good vinegar (or lemon juice) which vary in acidity from Balsamic vinegar to red and white wine vinegars to lemon juice. Use whichever best suits the flavor and clarity of the salad. Mustard is sometimes used in dressings to add flavor and aid in the emulsion of these sauces. Do not overdress the salad; this results in wilted, soggy greens. Dress just before serving and don't use all the dressing at once. Toss the greens gently to avoid bruising and taste them for seasonings and saucing. Add more of either if necessary.

These are the elements that create a delicious Italian salad: crisp, fresh greens, vegetables appropriately cut and blanched, and a sauce which marries the ingredients into a flavorful union of textures and colors. Served as a palate refresher and aid to digestion after any meal (and before dessert) insalata verde contributes color, fiber, and essential nutrients to the vegetarian diet.

RADICCHIO SALAD
Insalata di Radicchio

Native to the Veneto region of Italy, radicchio is a red lettuce that looks like a small cabbage. Because of its increasing popularity with American cooks, it can be found in many supermarkets as well as gourmet shops.

2 heads radicchio

2 heads Bibb lettuce

2 tablespoons finely chopped shallots

1 teaspoon Dijon mustard

2 teaspoons minced fresh basil

1 tablespoon Balsamic or red wine vinegar

¼ cup olive oil, preferably extra virgin

1 teaspoon salt

¼ teaspoon freshly ground pepper

Rinse the radicchio and Bibb lettuce and pat dry. Tear into 1-inch pieces (you'll have about 4 cups) and combine them in the salad bowl. In a separate bowl, whisk together the shallots, mustard, basil, and vinegar. Add the oil a little at a time, whisking constantly to emulsify the oil into the vinegar mixture. Season the dressing with half the salt and pepper.

Just before serving, lightly toss the salad with the dressing. Test for seasoning and add salt and pepper as necessary. Serve at once.
Serves 6. Preparation time: 15 minutes

JERUSALEM ARTICHOKE SALAD
Insalata di Topinambour

Jerusalem artichokes are a native of North America and a fairly recent addition to the Italian kitchen, adding their delicate flavor and crunchy texture to a variety of dishes. They are not artichokes at all but the roots of a variety of sunflower which grows all over northern Italy (perhaps accounting for this popularity). Well scrubbed or peeled, they can be cooked and puréed or eaten raw, as in this salad.

2 pounds Jerusalem artichokes
1 cup water
¼ cup white vinegar
1 bunch watercress, leaves only
2 tablespoons olive oil, preferably extra virgin
½ teaspoon salt
¼ teaspoon pepper

Peel the artichokes and slice thinly into coin-sized rounds. Place them in a bowl with the water and vinegar; set aside. Wash the cress leaves in cold water, pat dry, and transfer to the salad bowl. Just before serving, drain the sliced artichokes and add to the bowl. Toss with the olive oil, salt, and pepper. Taste, correct the seasoning if necessary and serve immediately.
Serves 6. Preparation time: 15 minutes

FRESH MOZZARELLA AND TOMATOES
Insalata di Mozzarella e Pomodori

This classic dish is best made with vine-ripened tomatoes, fresh basil, and freshly made mozzarella. It can be prepared 2 to 3 hours before serving, as either a salad or an appetizer.

3 medium firm tomatoes

8 ounces fresh mozzarella

3 tablespoons olive oil, preferably extra virgin

6 leaves fresh basil, coarsely chopped

1 teaspoon fresh oregano

½ teaspoon salt

¼ teaspoon freshly ground pepper

Peel the tomatoes and cut them in ½-inch thick slices. Slice the mozzarella ¼-inch thick. Layer the cheese and tomato slices alternately and slightly overlapping on a large plate. Drizzle with oil, and sprinkle the basil, oregano, salt, and pepper over all. Serve at room temperature. *Serves 6. Preparation time: 15 minutes*

SPINACH CAESAR SALAD
Insalata di Spinaci alla Cesare

Croutons:

¼ cup olive oil

1 garlic clove

2 cups ½-inch bread cubes, preferably Italian bread

Salad:

2 pounds fresh spinach, thoroughly washed and dried

1 large garlic clove

½ cup freshly grated parmesan

1 egg

1 teaspoon Dijon mustard

1 ½ tablespoons wine vinegar

¼ cup olive oil, preferably extra virgin

½ teaspoon salt

¼ teaspoon freshly ground pepper

To prepare the croutons, heat the olive oil in a medium skillet. Crush the garlic clove and sauté for 1 or 2 minutes, stirring often, to flavor the oil. Remove the garlic and sauté the bread cubes until golden, turning to brown each side. Remove with a slotted spoon and drain on crumpled paper towels; reserve.

Remove the stems from the spinach and tear the leaves into 2-inch pieces. Cut the garlic clove in half and rub the inside of a wooden salad bowl with it. Discard the garlic and place the spinach in the bowl; sprinkle with grated parmesan.

Coddle the egg by cooking it in barely simmering water for 1½ minutes. Remove from the pot and set aside. In a separate bowl, whisk together the mustard, vinegar, olive oil, salt, and pepper. Just before serving, toss the spinach with this dressing. Taste the salad and correct the seasoning if necessary. Break the egg over the salad and gently toss to mix well without bruising the greens. At the last minute, toss in the croutons and serve.

Serves 6. Preparation time: 25 minutes

 # FENNEL AND ARUGULA SALAD
Insalata di Finocchio e Ruchetta

Celery may be substituted if fennel is not available, but add a teaspoon of anise liqueur to the dressing to obtain the same flavor.

3 large fennel bulbs

3 cups arugula leaves

¼ cup olive oil, preferably extra virgin

1 tablespoon Balsamic or red wine vinegar

½ teaspoon salt

¼ teaspoon freshly ground pepper

Cut the stalks from the fennel and remove the outside layer of the bulb with a sharp vegetable peeler. Cut the bulb into quarters and core. Slice the quarters into thin crescents. Wash in cold water and drain on paper towels. Wash the arugula in cold water and pat dry. Combine the fennel and arugula in the salad bowl. In a separate bowl, beat together the oil, vinegar, salt, and pepper. Toss this dressing over the greens, check for seasoning, and serve.

Serves 6. Preparation time: 15 minutes

ORANGE AND FENNEL SALAD
Insalata di Arancia e Finocchio

4 navel oranges

2 large fennel bulbs

1 cup thinly sliced red onion

2 tablespoons lemon juice

¼ cup olive oil, preferably extra virgin

1 teaspoon salt

½ teaspoon freshly ground pepper

Peel the oranges, carefully cutting away all the white pith. Section them and remove the membranes from each segment. Cut the stalks from the fennel and trim the root ends. Cut the bulbs in half, remove the cores, and cut in thin slices. Toss all the ingredients together and allow to marinate in the refrigerator for at least 30 minutes, stirring once to blend the flavors. Serve at this point or cover and store in the refrigerator. The salad is best just slightly chilled.

Serves 6. Preparation time: 15 minutes

RADISH AND CUCUMBER SALAD
Insalata di Ravenelli e Cetrioli

Markets in Europe and the United States now feature a variety of radishes, including the Japanese daikon and black radish. These larger radishes can be sliced and spread with butter to make a simple appetizer. Here however, I prefer our common red radish, playing its peppery flavor against the coolness of cucumber.

1 pound radishes, well scrubbed

2 small cucumbers

1 tablespoon white wine vinegar

1 tablespoon olive oil, preferably extra virgin

1 teaspoon salt

¼ teaspoon freshly ground white pepper

Trim the ends from the radishes, cut them into thin slices, and place them in a salad bowl. Peel the cucumbers, halve them lengthwise, and scoop out their seeds. Cut the cucumbers into thin slices and add these to the radishes. In a small bowl, mix together the vinegar, oil, salt, and pepper. Pour the dressing over the vegetables and toss to coat them well. The salad can be served at this point, or allowed to marinate up to 4 hours, tossing occasionally.
Serves 6. Preparation time: 15 minutes

FONTINA SALAD WITH
CREAMY MUSTARD DRESSING
Insalata Fontina

3 bell peppers, preferably yellow, in 1-inch dice

24 very large green Sicilian olives, pitted and halved

⅔ cup Italian fontina in 1-inch dice

½ cup heavy cream

2 tablespoons Dijon mustard

3 tablespoons Balsamic or red wine vinegar

½ teaspoon salt

¼ teaspoon freshly ground pepper

3 tablespoons finely chopped broadleaf parsley

In the salad bowl, toss together the peppers, olives, and cheese. Whisk the cream with the mustard in a small bowl, then whisk in the vinegar and season with salt and pepper. Toss the salad with this dressing and taste for seasoning. Sprinkle with parsley and serve. The salad can be refrigerated (covered) but should be allowed to sit at room temperature for 10 minutes before serving.

Serves 6. Preparation time: 15 minutes

 # GREEN BEAN AND SCALLION SALAD
Insalata di Fagiolini e Cipolline

2 pounds green beans

1 red bell pepper

1 bunch scallions

¼ cup olive oil

2 tablespoons white wine vinegar

1 teaspoon salt

¼ teaspoon freshly ground pepper

6 lettuce leaves, preferably Boston, Romaine, or Bibb

Bring a large pot of salted water to boil. As the water heats, wash the vegetables in cold running water and string the beans if necessary. Cook the beans for 2 to 4 minutes, until they are tender but still firm. Immediately refresh them in cold water and drain when cool. Transfer the beans to a large bowl. Slice the scallions into thin rounds and add to the beans. Core and seed the red pepper; slice it into six ¼-inch thick rounds and set aside.

In a small bowl, mix the olive oil, vinegar, salt, and pepper until well blended. Toss this dressing with the beans and scallions. Place the lettuce leaves on 6 plates. Arrange the beans in 6 neat bundles, slipping a pepper ring around each. Carefully set the bundles on the lettuce and serve. The salads can be kept in the refrigerator, but do cover them with plastic wrap to prevent the lettuce wilting.

Serves 6. Preparation time: 25 minutes

WATERCRESS SALAD WITH MUSHROOMS AND GRUYERE
Insalata Verushka

2 cups firm, tightly closed mushrooms
¼ cup lemon juice
1 bunch watercress
1½ cups celery, peeled and sliced thinly on the bias
½ pound gruyere, in ⅛-inch by 1½-inch strips
½ cup plus 1 tablespoon olive oil, preferably
    extra virgin
½ teaspoon salt
¼ teaspoon freshly ground pepper

Wipe the mushrooms with a damp cloth or paper towel, trim the stems, and cut into thin slices. Toss the mushrooms with 1 tablespoon of the lemon juice to prevent discoloration. Wash the cress in cold water and pat dry. Remove the leaves from the stems (which can be used to flavor a vegetable stock). Combine the sliced mushrooms, cress, and celery with the gruyere in a salad bowl. In a separate bowl, whisk together the remaining 3 tablespoons of lemon juice, the olive oil, salt, and pepper. Pour the dressing over the salad, toss, and serve. *Serves 6. Preparation time: 20 minutes*

ASPARAGUS AND EGG SALAD
Insalata di Asparagi e Uova

Asparagus is available in different sizes, from the pencil-thin variety to the ½-inch thick spears more often seen in the market. It will cook more evenly if you peel thick spears to remove the tough skin and trim away the woody ends of the stalks. When cooking asparagus, test it frequently to detect that moment when the raw taste is gone but the stalks are still slightly crunchy; thin asparagus will take less than a minute. Quickly refresh the asparagus in cold water to stop the cooking process at this point.

2 pounds asparagus, peeled and trimmed

3 hard-cooked eggs

2 tablespoons capers, rinsed and drained

2 tablespoons minced broadleaf parsley

2 tablespoons lemon juice

½ teaspoon Dijon mustard

½ cup olive oil, preferably extra virgin

½ teaspoon salt

¼ teaspoon freshly ground pepper

Steam the asparagus over salted boiling water or cook it in lots of salted boiling water until just tender but still firm to the bite. This will take 1 to 5 minutes, depending on its thickness. Lift out the asparagus with a slotted spoon and immediately refresh in cold running water. Drain the cooled asparagus, transfer to a bowl, and reserve.

Separate the egg yolks from the whites and chop the whites. Toss the whites with the capers and parsley. Mash the yolks in a small bowl and mix in the lemon juice. With a fork, gradually beat in the oil, blending well and emulsifying the oil into the egg mixture. Add ½ teaspoon of salt and the pepper. Toss 1 tablespoon of the sauce with the caper mixture. Toss the remaining sauce with the asparagus; taste for salt and add more if necessary. Arrange the asparagus on a chilled serving platter or individual salad plates and sprinkle the caper mixture in a band over it. The salad can be served at once or chilled.

Serves 6. Preparation time: 30 minutes

RICE-STUFFED TOMATOES
Pomodori al Riso

This dish requires the freshest, ripest red tomatoes you can find. I make it only in the summer when locally grown produce is at its peak.

1½ cups water

1 cup rice, preferably Arborio

1 teaspoon salt

⅛ teaspoon freshly ground pepper

6 large, firm, ripe tomatoes

1 teaspoon vegetable oil

½ cup plus 2 teaspoons olive oil

2 garlic cloves, minced

2 tablespoons minced fresh basil

1 teaspoon minced fresh mint

3 tablespoons minced fresh broadleaf parsley

Bring the water to boil in a medium saucepan. Stir in the rice and season with salt and pepper. Cover the pan and turn heat to low. Cook the rice until all the liquid is absorbed, about 18 to 20 minutes.

Meanwhile, core the stem ends of the tomatoes. Cut off and reserve ½-inch tops. Carefully scoop out the pulp and remove the seeds. Chop the pulp and place it with its juices in a mixing bowl.

Preheat the oven to 375°. Oil a baking pan large enough to hold the tomatoes and set aside. Turn the cooked rice into the mixing bowl with the tomato pulp and toss to mix. Add the ½ cup olive oil, garlic, and herbs, and continue to toss until the ingredients are well-distributed. Fill the tomato shells with the seasoned rice and replace the tops. Set each in the oiled baking pan and drizzle a little olive oil over the tops. Bake for 30 minutes, until the tomatoes are just tender and the rice heated through. Serve immediately.
Serves 6. Preparation time: 1 hour

CAULIFLOWER WITH FRESH HERB SAUCE
Cavolfiore con Salsa Verde

Choose a firm, white, unblemished cauliflower for this dish as it makes a very attractive presentation. The florets are cooked separately, then reformed into a head by packing them tightly into a round bowl.

1½ cups Fresh Herb Sauce (Page 55)

1 tablespoon vegetable oil

1 large head cauliflower

¼ cup lemon juice

1 tablespoon salt

¼ cup toasted breadcrumbs

1 tablespoon olive oil

Make or reheat the sauce and keep warm. Oil an oven-proof bowl with a rounded bottom. Preheat the oven to 350°.

Remove and discard the outside leaves and core of the cauliflower. Separate the cauliflower into florets with stems about ½-inch long. Try to keep the florets whole unless they are very large.

Bring several quarts of water to a boil and stir in the lemon juice and salt. Add the cauliflower and cook for about 5 minutes, until just tender when pierced with a small, sharp knife. Drain the cauliflower and rinse well with cold water. Reform the head in the prepared bowl, placing the florets end-down and packing tightly. When the sides of the bowl are filled, place the remaining florets in the center, keeping the top of the layer as flat and even as possible.

Place the bowl in the oven until ready to serve, but no longer than 10 minutes or the cauliflower will overcook. Unmold the cauliflower by inverting it onto a serving platter. (Any florets that slip out can be tucked back in.) Spoon a ring of herb sauce around the base of the cauliflower. Toss the breadcrumbs with the olive oil and sprinkle over the top of the cauliflower. Serve immediately, passing the rest of the sauce separately.

Serves 6. Preparation time: 25 minutes

SPICY CHICK PEA SALAD
Insalata di Ceci fra Diavolo

1 pound chick peas, soaked overnight, or 2 16-ounce
    cans chick peas, drained

1 pound plum tomatoes or 1 32-ounce can
    plum tomatoes, drained, peeled, seeded, and
    coarsely chopped

½ cup chopped bell pepper

½ cup chopped red onion

3 tablespoons Balsamic or red wine vinegar

½ cup olive oil, preferably extra virgin

1 teaspoon chopped hot chili pepper, or 1 teaspoon
    red pepper flakes

1 garlic clove, minced

½ teaspoon salt

¼ cup minced broadleaf parsley

Cook dried chick peas in 2 quarts of salted water until tender, about 1½ hours. Drain the peas and allow to cool. In a large bowl, combine the cooked or canned chick peas with the tomatoes, pepper, and onion; set aside. In a separate bowl, combine the vinegar, oil, chili pepper, garlic, and salt, and beat with a fork until well blended. Pour the pepper sauce over the chick peas, toss until the ingredients are evenly distributed, and taste for seasoning. Just before serving, toss in the parsley. This salad will keep in the refrigerator, but is better served at room temperature or slightly chilled.

Serves 6. Preparation time (not including cooking chick peas): 25 minutes

CHAPTER 11

BREADS

There is nothing to compare with the aroma and taste of fresh home-baked bread; fresh from the oven, still warm enough to melt butter, it is all too easy to find a whole loaf disappearing in minutes. For such a simple food, homemade bread adds so much to any meal—be it a fresh soup and salad, a simple frittata, or as part of a full dinner party.

Dozens of books have been written on bread, and the recipes that follow represent only a sample of the many types of Italian bread. In all cases, they have been selected with an eye to the less experienced baker while at the same time presenting a variety in a limited space. My recipe for Italian Bread provides a base for the four flavored breads that follow. Once mastered, you can experiment with your own seasonings. The pepper bread sticks are from a classic recipe and can be served to accompany an appetizer or alone as a snack, with a glass of wine. Gorgonzola crackers make surprisingly light savory snacks and antipasto. The dough is very versatile and can be used equally as a crust for a torta filled with vegetables or eggs which I serve as a main dish.

Panettone is the traditional Italian Christmas cake, originally from Milan but now made throughout Italy. Commercial versions of this sweet bread can be found in this country, but it is far better fresh-baked. Amaretti, also well-known here, are only one of the many sweet cookies eaten with a cup of espresso as a snack or at the end of a meal. The sweet biscuits and rusks are both easy to keep to serve as you would other cookies or after dinner.

ITALIAN BREAD WITH OLIVE OIL
Pane all'Olio

This dough produces a crusty loaf with the subtle flavor of olives.

2 packages active dry yeast

1 cup warm water

3 cups flour, approximately

1 teaspoon salt

1 tablespoon olive oil, preferably extra virgin, plus

   1 teaspoon for bowl

Sprinkle the yeast in ½ cup warm water (105° to 115°), stir to dissolve, and set in a warm place for 5 minutes. Put 1½ cups of flour onto a work surface and make a well in the center. Pour the yeast mixture into the well and work in the flour gradually, pulling in flour from the sides of the well. When all the flour is incorporated, bring the dough together in a ball and knead for 8 minutes. Knead by pushing the dough forward with the palm of your hand and folding back the far edge with your fingers. Turn the dough a quarter turn after each knead. Keep the top of the dough and the work surface lightly sprinkled with flour so that the dough does not stick.

If your mixer has a dough hook attachment, you can use it to knead the dough. Or, you can prepare the dough in a food processor: place the dry ingredients in the work bowl and with the machine running, add the yeast mixture. The dough needs only 5 minutes kneading with this method.

When you have a smooth, elastic dough, place it in a bowl brushed with olive oil and cover with a clean, damp cloth. Allow to rise in a warm (75° to 80°), draught-free spot until the dough is doubled in bulk, about 1½ hours.

Punch the dough down. Put 1½ cups of flour on the work surface and make a well in it. Pour the remaining ½ cup of water into the well, add the salt and the olive oil, and place the dough in the center. Work these ingredients together so that, again, you have a smooth, elastic ball, kneading for about 8 minutes. Place the dough in a clean, oiled bowl, cover, and allow to rise again until doubled in bulk, 1½ hours approximately.

Preheat the oven to 425°. Turn the dough out onto the lightly floured work surface and knead it for 1 minute to release any air bubbles. Shape the dough into a long loaf or a round, or divide it in half and shape into 2 smaller loaves. Dust the top with flour. As decoration, you may want to make several shallow slashes across the top, using a sharp knife or a razor. Place the dough on a lightly oiled baking sheet and bake for 45 minutes. The bread is done when tapping on the crust produces a hollow sound. The bread can be eaten warm, but do allow it to cool slightly on a rack before serving.

Makes 1 large, or 2 small loaves. Preparation time: About 4½ hours

 # GARLIC TOASTS
Bruschetta

Bruschetta is a crusty, toasted version of garlic bread. Traditionally it is grilled over hot coals, but an oven broiler can be used. Make these garlic toasts with the finest quality olive oil you have.

12 to 15 slices Italian bread, ½-inch thick
2 large garlic cloves, halved
½ cup olive oil, preferably extra virgin
1 tablespoon Balsamic or red wine vinegar (optional)

Prepare the grill or preheat the broiler. Rub one side of each slice of bread with a cut side of garlic clove. Brush the bread with olive oil, then the vinegar if desired. Grill the bread 5-inches from the heat until lightly browned on both sides, turning once. Serve immediately.

Serves 6. Preparation time: 10 minutes

OLIVE OIL AND HERB BREAD
Pane all'Olio e Condimenti

Dough:

¼ teaspoon sugar

2 cups warm water

1 package active dry yeast

1 tablespoon salt

5½ cups sifted flour, approximately

2 teaspoons olive oil

Filling:

1 tablespoon chopped fresh basil

½ teaspoon rosemary

½ teaspoon sage

½ teaspoon oregano

¼ teaspoon freshly ground pepper

¼ cup olive oil

Dissolve the sugar in ¼ cup warm water (105°–115°). Sprinkle the yeast into the water, stir to dissolve, and allow to sit for 5 or 10 minutes, until the mixture begins to foam. When the yeast is bubbly, combine the remaining warm water and the salt in a large mixing bowl, then blend in 3 cups of flour. Stir the softened yeast and pour into the flour, mixing to blend well. When the dough is smooth, add 1 cup of flour and continue to stir until smooth again. Continue to add flour until you have a soft dough that is just slightly sticky. Shape the dough into a ball and turn out onto a lightly floured work surface. Cover with an inverted bowl large enough so that it does not touch the dough; allow to rest 10 minutes.

Knead the dough until smooth and elastic, about 5 to 8 minutes, sprinkling with flour to prevent sticking. Shape the dough into a smooth ball and place it in a large bowl brushed with olive oil, turning once to coat the top with oil. Cover the bowl with wax paper and a towel and allow the dough to rise in a warm (75° to 80°), draught-free place until doubled in bulk, about 1½ hours. When the dough has doubled, punch it down, knead on a lightly floured surface for 2 minutes, and cut it in half. Shape each half into a ball, cover these with a towel, and let rest for 10 minutes.

 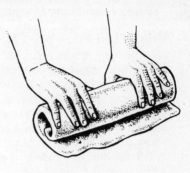

1 Roll out half the dough on a lightly floured surface. Coat with olive oil to within 1-inch of the edges then sprinkle evenly with the herbs.

2 Gently roll the dough, starting at the longer end, into a loaf.

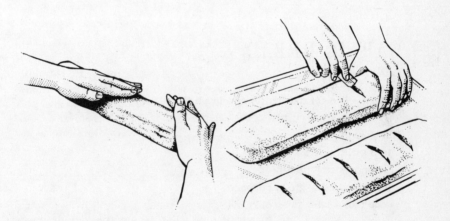

3 Pinch and turn under the ends to seal the loaf and place seam side down on a baking sheet.

4 With a sharp knife or razor make diagonal slashes across the top, then cover and allow to rise in a warm place until doubled in bulk.

Prepare the filling by combining all of the ingredients except the olive oil; set aside. Lightly oil a baking sheet. Roll each portion of dough to an 8-inch by 14-inch rectangle. Coat the surface of each up to 1-inch of the edges with olive oil, then sprinkle with the mixed herbs. Starting at the longer edge, gently roll the dough into a long, slender loaf. Pinch and turn under the ends to seal and place seam-side down on the baking sheet. Repeat for the second loaf, placing it alongside the first. With a razor or sharp knife, make 3 shallow diagonal slashes across the top of each loaf. Cover loosely with a towel and allow to rise in a warm place until doubled in bulk, about 45 minutes.

Fifteen minutes before the loaves are ready, preheat the oven to 425°. Bake the bread for 10 minutes, then reduce the heat to 350° and bake 1 hour. To make the crusts especially crispy, place a pan of boiling water on the bottom rack of the oven as the bread is baking.

Cool the loaves on a rack before serving.

Makes 2 loaves. Preparation time: 4½ hours

GARLIC BREAD
Pane all'Aglio

1 recipe Olive Oil and Herb Bread dough (Page 164)

Filling:
6 to 8 garlic cloves
½ teaspoon fresh oregano
1 teaspoon freshly ground pepper
¼ cup plus 1 tablespoon olive oil

Follow the method for Olive Oil and Herb Bread (Page 164). Prepare the filling while the dough is resting for 10 minutes after the first rising. Boil the garlic cloves in their skins for 10 minutes. Peel and mash them into a paste, adding the oregano, pepper, and 1 tablespoon of olive oil. Lightly oil a baking sheet and roll out the dough, as directed. After coating the dough with the ¼ cup of olive oil, spread half the garlic mixture on each loaf. Follow the directions to shape and bake the bread.

Makes 2 loaves. Preparation time: 4½ hours

ROSEMARY BREAD
Pan di Rosmarino

2 tablespoons olive oil, preferably extra virgin
1 tablespoon minced fresh rosemary
1 teaspoon sugar
1½ cups warm water
2 packages active dry yeast
3 cups flour, approximately
½ teaspoon salt
2 teaspoons vegetable oil

Heat the olive oil and gently sauté the rosemary for 3 minutes, until fragrant; cool to lukewarm. Dissolve the sugar in ¼ cup of warm water (105° to 115°); sprinkle in the yeast and stir to dissolve. Set in a warm place to proof for 5 minutes. Put 2½ cups of flour on your work surface and make a well in the center. Pour in the yeast and cooled rosemary oil and incorporate them into the flour with your fingertips. Gradually add the remaining warm water, working it in to make a smooth dough. Knead the dough, sprinkling with flour to keep it from sticking, until it is smooth and elastic, about 8 minutes, and shape into a ball. Brush a bowl with vegetable oil and place the dough in it, turning once to coat the top with oil. Cover with a damp cloth and allow to rise in a warm place for 1 hour, until doubled in bulk.

Punch down the dough and knead it for 1 minute to release any air bubbles. Oil a baking sheet or loaf pan with the rest of the vegetable oil. Form the dough into 1 round or 2 long loaves, or into a shape that will fit into the loaf pan. Transfer the dough to the pan, cover loosely, and allow to rest for 20 minutes.

Preheat the oven to 400°. Dust the dough with flour and make 3 diagonal slashes across the top. Place the pan in the oven and immediately reduce the heat to 350°. Bake until golden brown, about 45 minutes for 1 large loaf or 30 minutes for 2 smaller loaves. Allow to cool on a rack.

Makes 1 large or 2 small loaves. Preparation time: 2½ hours

PEPPER BREAD STICKS
Grissini

Bread sticks are a specialty of Turin, and these are spiced with lots of freshly ground pepper. For variety the dough can be shaped into little round biscuits; snip a cross on the top of each with scissors before baking. Brushing with a beaten egg before baking will give them a shiny, golden crust.

1 package active dry yeast

1¼ cups warm water

½ cup olive oil, preferably extra virgin

4 cups flour, approximately

1 teaspoon sugar

1½ teaspoons salt

1 tablespoon freshly ground pepper

½ teaspoon aniseed

2 teaspoons oil

1 egg (optional)

1 cup freshly grated parmesan or
    1 cup sesame seeds (optional)

Sprinkle the yeast in ¼ cup warm (105°–115°) water and stir to dissolve. Allow the yeast to proof in a warm place for 10 minutes. Mix the remaining water with ½ cup of the olive oil; reserve. Put 3½ cups of flour in a large bowl and make a well in the center. Place the sugar, salt, pepper, and aniseed in the well, then pour in the yeast, water, and oil. Stir the liquid into the flour with a wooden spoon. When the dough is too stiff to stir, turn it out onto a lightly floured work surface and knead it for 8 minutes, adding more flour as necessary. Brush a large bowl with olive oil. Shape the dough into a smooth ball and place it in the bowl, turning once to coat the top with oil. Cover the bowl with a damp cloth and allow the dough to rise in a warm, draught-free place until doubled in bulk, about 1 hour.

Lightly oil 2 baking sheets and set aside. Punch down the dough and knead it for 1 minute to release any air bubbles. Divide the dough into 36 pieces fairly equal in size. On a lightly floured surface, roll each piece into a stick about 10-inches long. (If you are making biscuits, shape the pieces into balls and flatten slightly with your hand.) Brush each with lightly beaten egg, if desired. Roll the sticks in grated parmesan or sesame seeds. Arrange them on the baking sheets and allow to rest for 30 minutes. Meanwhile, preheat the oven to 400°.

Bake the sticks (or biscuits) for 20 minutes. Remove them from the baking sheets and allow to cool on racks. Serve the bread sticks warm or allow to cool and store.
Makes 36 sticks. Preparation time: 2 hours

 # GORGONZOLA CRACKERS
Pizzette al Gorgonzola

These crisp, delicious crackers can be served with an aperitif or as a snack at any time. The dough also makes a superb crust for turnovers or savory tarts such as Spinach Pie (Page 130).

½ cup plus 1 teaspoon butter, at room temperature
½ pound gorgonzola, crumbled, at room temperature
2½ cups flour
1 teaspoon salt
⅛ teaspoon freshly ground pepper
3 egg yolks
2 tablespoons milk

Cream together ½ cup of the butter and the gorgonzola until smooth and homogenous. Mix the dry ingredients together on your work surface and make a well in the center. Place the creamed butter and cheese and the egg yolks in the well and gradually work in the flour. To distribute the flour and cheese evenly, shape the dough into a ball and, using the heel of your hand, push the dough down and forward a little at a time. Turn the dough over and repeat the process. Shape the dough into a ball again and wrap tightly in foil or plastic wrap. Refrigerate for at least 30 minutes.

Preheat the oven to 400° and butter a baking sheet. Roll out the dough on a floured surface to ¼-inch thickness. Using a scalloped cookie cutter or floured glass, cut 2-inch rounds. Place the rounds on the baking sheet, then gather up and reroll the dough scraps to cut more. Brush the rounds with a light coat of milk and bake on the middle rack of the preheated oven for 15 minutes, turning the baking sheet if necessary for the crackers to brown evenly. Cool on a rack.
Makes 48 crackers. Preparation time: 1 hour

PANETTONE

Traditionally served at Christmas, panettone is a rich sweet bread studded with raisins, toasted pine nuts, and candied lemon peel.

2 packages active dry yeast

¼ cup warm water

¼ cup milk

¼ cup plus 2 teaspoons butter

¾ cup plus 1 teaspoon sugar

¾ teaspoon salt

Grated rind of 1 large lemon

1 teaspoon vanilla

3 cups flour, approximately

1 egg

2 egg yolks

1 teaspoon vegetable oil

⅓ cup raisins

⅓ cup sultana raisins

¼ cup chopped candied lemon peel or citron

¼ cup lightly toasted pine nuts

Sprinkle the yeast into the warm (105°–115°) water, stir to dissolve, and set in a warm place for 10 minutes. Scald the milk and remove from the heat. Add the ¼ cup of butter, stirring constantly until it is melted. Pour this mixture into a large bowl and add ¾ cup of sugar, the salt, lemon rind, and vanilla. Stir in the yeast and 2 cups of flour. Add the egg and 1 yolk and stir to blend well. Work in the remaining flour gradually and when the dough is too stiff to stir, turn it onto a lightly floured surface and knead by hand. Knead the dough until it is smooth and elastic, about 8 minutes, sprinkling with flour to prevent sticking. Shape the dough into a ball. Brush a bowl with oil and place the dough in it, turning once to coat the top. Cover the bowl with a damp cloth and set it in a warm place to rise for 2 hours.

While the dough is rising, plump the raisins in hot water for 30 minutes. Drain and pat dry on paper towels. Butter a 6-inch charlotte mold and line the bottom and sides with parchment or wax paper. Turn the dough out onto a floured surface and knead in the raisins, lemon peel, and nuts. Place the dough in the prepared mold and cover with a cloth. Set the mold in a warm place for at least 8 hours or overnight, until the dough has risen to form a rounded balloon over the top of the mold.

Preheat the oven to 400° and position a rack in the lowest setting (remove the other racks). Mix the remaining egg yolk with 1 teaspoon of sugar. Carefully brush the top of the dough with this glaze, making sure that the entire surface is coated, and set in the preheated oven. After 10 minutes, reduce the heat to 350° and continue to bake for 45 minutes. If the crust browns too quickly, place a piece of foil over it. Allow the bread to rest for 15 minutes after baking, then unmold and remove the paper casing. Panettone can be served warm; to store, allow to cool completely and wrap well. It can also be cut into thin slices and toasted.

Makes 1 bread. Preparation time (not including rising): 2 hours

 # BREAKFAST BREAD
Ciambella

Ciambella is a ring-shaped cake made all over Italy with almost as many variations as there are households. Though many of the sweets in Italy are bought in the pastry shop, this is an easy recipe to make at home. Its texture lends itself to dunking in breakfast coffee or milk, and it is also delicious spread with fresh, sweet butter.

6 tablespoons plus 1 teaspoon butter, at
   room temperature
¾ cup sugar
4 eggs

1 teaspoon vanilla

4 cups sifted flour

2 teaspoons baking powder

1 cup coarsely chopped walnuts

1 cup currants

Preheat the oven to 375° and butter a baking sheet. Cream the butter in a mixing bowl and beat in the sugar. Add the eggs one at a time, beating well after each addition. Beat in the vanilla. Sift the flour and baking powder into the bowl and mix well. Stir in the chopped walnuts and currants.

On the prepared baking sheet, shape the dough into a 10-inch ring with your hands (it should be quite thick). Bake for 35 minutes, until a toothpick inserted comes out clean and dry. Cool on a rack or serve while still warm.

Makes 1 ring. Preparation time: 1 hour

 # ALMOND MACAROONS
Amaretti

Traditionally, amaretti are made with a combination of sweet and bitter almonds. Bitter almonds are toxic, however, and are not available for baking in this country. Although macaroons are often made with marzipan and have a shiny, cracked appearance, these are made with ground almonds for a more homemade look. Sprinkle them with confectioners' sugar before baking for a light glaze.

1 tablespoon butter

2 cups finely ground almonds

⅔ cup sugar

4 or 5 egg whites

½ teaspoon vanilla

Confectioners' sugar (optional)

Preheat the oven to 350° and butter 2 baking sheets. Grind the almonds again with the sugar, by hand, or in a blender or food processor. Lightly beat the egg whites with the vanilla. Then gradually add them to the almonds, blending well after each addition and checking the consistency of the mixture: to make macaroon 'kisses', a relatively thick batter is needed. Spoon the batter into a pastry bag fitted with a large star tube and pipe 'kisses' about 1½-inches in diameter at 1-inch intervals on the baking sheets. (I prefer flatter macaroons, and add enough whites to make a smooth batter. This forms a plump 2-inch round when 1 tablespoon of the batter is dropped onto the baking sheet.)

Sift confectioners' sugar over the cookies if desired. Bake the macaroons for about 20 minutes, until lightly browned, turning the sheets so that the cookies brown evenly. When they are done, transfer the baking sheets to a cooling rack and allow the macaroons to stand for 5 minutes. Use a spatula to remove the cookies from the sheets and continue to cool on racks.

Makes 24 macaroons. Preparation time: 35 minutes

ALMOND SHORTBREAD
Biscotto di Mandorle

This biscotto is a large cookie broken into pieces to serve. Pass it after the meal with a sweet wine or with an ice cream or sherbet.

1 cup plus 1 teaspoon butter, at room temperature
2 cups flour
1 cup finely ground almonds
¾ cup sugar
1 teaspoon grated lemon rind
2 tablespoons lemon juice

Preheat the oven to 350°, and butter a baking sheet with the extra teaspoon. Cream the cup of butter in a large mixing bowl until it is light and fluffy. Combine the flour, ground almonds, sugar, and lemon rind, and gradually cream these into the butter about ½ cup at a time, beating well after each addition. Beat in the lemon juice.

Gather the dough into a ball and place on the baking sheet. With a rolling pin or by hand, flatten the dough to an 8-inch round, about 1½-inches thick. Lightly crimp the edges with a fork and score the top with the back of a knife into 8 pie-shaped wedges. Bake for 40 minutes, until golden on top and lightly browned at the edges. Carefully transfer the shortbread to a rack and allow to cool.
Serves 8. Preparation time: 50 minutes

HAZELNUT RUSKS
Biscotti alla Nocciola

The hazelnuts need not be peeled for this recipe as the skins add a toasted flavor to the cookies.

½ cup plus 1 teaspoon butter, at room temperature
2 eggs
1 teaspoon vanilla
1 cup finely chopped hazelnuts
2 cups flour

½ teaspoon baking powder

⅔ cup sugar

1 tablespoon finely chopped candied orange peel or

   1 tablespoon grated orange rind

Cream the butter in a large bowl until smooth. Add 1 egg and beat until well blended; stir in the vanilla. Combine the hazelnuts, flour, baking powder, sugar, and candied peel or grated rind. Gradually beat them, about ½ cup at a time, into the butter, mixing well after each addition. Divide the dough in half. Shape each portion into a long rounded loaf, 3-inches by 8-inches. It should be rounded at the sides and slightly higher in the middle, tapering off toward the sides. Wrap the loaves in wax paper or plastic wrap and chill in the refrigerator for at least 30 minutes.

Preheat the oven to 350° and butter a baking sheet. Lightly beat the remaining egg. Unwrap the loaves and place them on the baking sheet. Brush the tops and sides with the beaten egg and score the top of the loaves at ¾-inch intervals. Bake for 1 hour, turning the sheet once to ensure even browning, until the loaves are golden brown and dry. If they begin to brown too quickly, lightly cover them with foil. Remove from the oven and allow the loaves to cool on racks for 5 minutes. Cut the warm loaves in ¾-inch slices, and serve warm or allow to cool completely and store.

Makes 12 to 15 rusks. Preparation time: 1¾ hours

WINE BISCUITS
Biscotti di Vino

½ cup plus 1 tablespoon butter, at room temperature

½ cup sugar

2 eggs

½ teaspoon vanilla

3 cups flour

2 teaspoons baking powder

⅛ teaspoon salt

½ cup Marsala

Cream the butter in a mixing bowl and gradually add ½ cup of the sugar, beating until light. Add the eggs, one at a time, then the vanilla, beating well after each addition. Sift 2 cups of the flour, the baking powder, and the salt into the creamed butter; stir to blend. Stir in ¼ cup of the Marsala. Sift the remaining flour over the dough and stir it in, then add the remaining Marsala. Turn the dough out onto a work surface and divide it in half. With each portion, spread the dough evenly over 12-inch sheets of plastic wrap or wax paper. Roll the dough into long oval cylinders 1-inch high and 2-inches wide, about 8-inches long. Twist the ends of the wrap to seal and refrigerate for at least 30 minutes.

Preheat the oven to 375°. Butter 2 baking sheets with the remaining tablespoon or line them with parchment paper. Unwrap the chilled dough and cut into ¼-inch thick slices. Arrange the slices on the baking sheets (the dough should not spread). Bake until the biscuits are golden brown, about 12 to 15 minutes, and cool on racks.

Makes 60 cookies. Preparation time: 1 hour

CHAPTER 12

DESSERTS

More properly, this chapter should be titled "Desserts and Pastries" as I have included recipes for a few of the most popular confections for which Italian pastry chefs are renowned. Generally these pastries, filled with a rich, often almond or vanilla cream, are enjoyed like ices in cafes or bars rather than at the dinner table. Fresh fruit with or without cheese normally ends the Italian meal. On special occasions, however, or for larger meals, a sweet dessert will be served. A Zuppa Inglese or the cream-topped Monte Bianco would provide a dramatic finale for any gathering or celebration. For those whose sweet tooth does not extend to Italian pastries or who are looking for something a little less ostentatious than Zuppa Inglese, I have included fresh fruit tarts and poached and stuffed fruit recipes.

Short Pastry Dough can be used equally for savory tarts and sweet. I sometimes fill it with eggs, cheese, and vegetables such as leeks, onions, tomatoes, mushrooms, escarole or artichokes, and add a variety of fresh herbs when plentiful. Serve it as an entrée with a green salad. The Sweet Short Pastry, however, is a versatile crust for any number of desserts: filled pastries, cheesecakes, and fruit tarts. Vanilla and ground almonds add their distinctive flavors to this pastry, which when baked can be filled with either of the two creams that follow as well as nuts and fresh fruits such as strawberries, grapes, peaches, or raspberries.

Cannoli are probably the most popular Italian pastries. Sinfully rich, these pastry tubes are fried to a crisp, then filled with a flavored cream. The ends are sprinkled with chopped nuts or candied peel. Fresh candied peel has a far superior flavor and texture to store-bought, and I have included a basic recipe for making it at home.

SHORT PASTRY
Pasta Frolla

This pastry is light and flaky (don't overwork the dough or it will toughen) and can be used in sweet or savory tarts. I always like to prebake the shell before adding a filling, but this step can be omitted if the pie is baked on the bottom shelf of a hot (425°) oven for the first 15 minutes.

2 cups flour

6 tablespoons cold butter, cut in pieces

2 tablespoons vegetable shortening

¾ teaspoon salt

¼ to ⅓ cup cold water

Place the flour in a mound on your work surface. Make a well in the center and place the butter, shortening, and salt in it. Work the fat into the flour with your fingertips until the butter is in pea-size lumps. Pour in the water a little at a time and fluff it in with your fingers. (Add only enough water to make the flour slightly damp.) Gather the dough in a ball in front of you. Working with a small amount at the far edge of the ball, press down and forward with the heel of your hand, sliding the dough away and against the work surface. Repeat four or five times until all the dough has been mixed. Turn the dough over and around and knead again. This process forms long, thin sheets of butter in the dough, which will make the pastry flaky.

To make the dough in a food processor, put the flour and salt in the work bowl and place the butter and shortening on top. With five or six pulses, chop the butter into the flour until it is in pea-size lumps. With the machine running, pour in just enough water until the dough comes together in one piece. Then work the dough as above.

Shape the dough into a ball and wrap tightly; refrigerate for at least 20 minutes before rolling out. Roll out the dough on a lightly floured surface, working away from the center in all directions, and turning the dough from time to time to prevent sticking. Or you can roll the dough between two sheets of parchment or wax paper.

Makes 1 10-inch pie or quiche shell. Preparation time: 20 minutes

SWEET SHORT PASTRY
Pasta Frolla per Crostata

This delicious sweet pastry is almost a cookie crust. Use a prebaked shell for a fresh fruit tart or cook it with a filling. The sugar and eggs can sometimes make this a moist dough to work with, so you may need to sprinkle a little flour over it to roll out.

1½ cups flour

½ cup cold butter, cut in pieces

3 tablespoons sugar

½ teaspoon vanilla

¼ teaspoon salt

¼ cup ground almonds

1 egg, beaten

Place the flour in a mound on a work surface and make a well in the center. In the well, place the butter, sugar, salt, vanilla, almonds, and the beaten egg. Proceed by hand or with a food processor according to the directions for Short Pastry on Page opposite. Wrap the dough and chill for at least 30 minutes before using.

Makes a 2 crust 9-inch pie, or 2 9-inch pie shells. Preparation time: 20 minutes

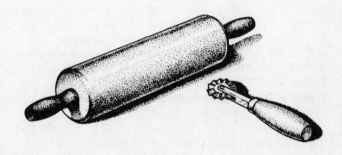

PASTRY CREAM
Crema Pasticciera

This rich, versatile pastry cream is flavored with rum, so popular with Italian pastry chefs, but you can also use Grand Marnier or brandy. As the cream is made with cornstarch it will not become soupy at room temperature, and so is easy to work with. Use it as a filling for cannoli or crespelle, or serve it alone with fresh fruit or macaroons.

5 tablespoons cornstarch

2 cups heavy cream

3 egg yolks

¼ cup sugar

1 tablespoon dark rum

1 teaspoon vanilla

A pinch of salt

3 ounces bittersweet chocolate, in pieces (optional)

Mix the cornstarch with ¼ cup of the heavy cream until smooth. Bring the remaining cream to a boil in the top of a double boiler or a heavy saucepan, making sure that it does not boil over. Cover and keep warm. Mix together the eggs and sugar, and whisk until glossy and lemon-colored, about 3 minutes. Stir in the rum, vanilla, and salt. Whisk in the cornstarch mixture. Gradually add the hot cream, whisking constantly. Pour the mixture back into the pan and cook over medium heat or simmering water, whisking constantly, until the cream thickens, about 3 minutes. Do not allow the cream to boil.

For chocolate pastry cream, add the chocolate now, whisking until it is melted and blended into the cream. If the cream begins to separate, immediately remove it from the heat and beat with an electric mixer or whisk until it is smooth again.

Pour the cream into a clean bowl and cover the surface with plastic wrap to prevent a crust from forming. Cool to room temperature, then refrigerate until ready to use.

Makes 2 cups. Preparation time: 20 minutes

ALMOND PASTRY CREAM
Crema alla Mandorle

This variation of Pastry Cream can be used uncooked as a filling or baked as a custard base for a fresh fruit tart. (If you plan to bake it, the pastry cream need not be cooled before adding the other ingredients.)

½ cup cold Pastry Cream (Page 180)

½ cup confectioners' sugar

⅔ cup ground blanched almonds

½ teaspoon vanilla

2 tablespoons softened butter

1 egg, beaten

1 tablespoon dark rum (optional)

Combine all the ingredients in a mixing bowl and blend well. Cover and keep refrigerated; use as desired.
Makes 1½ cups. Preparation time: 25 minutes

 # ZABAGLIONE

'Zabaglione' or 'zabaione', a dessert popular all over the world, is flavored with the sweet fortified Marsala wine from Sicily. A drier white wine can also be used, but be sure that it has a full bouquet to give the cream distinction.

6 egg yolks

6 tablespoons sugar

½ cup Marsala

Grated rind of 1 large orange

1 tablespoon vanilla

½ cup heavy cream

2 cups raspberries or other fresh fruit (optional)

Place the egg yolks in a heat-proof bowl or the top of a double boiler off the heat. Whisk to break them up, then add the sugar in a steady stream, whisking constantly. Beat to the ribbon stage: when it is lemon-colored and falls from the whisk in a glossy ribbon, about 5 to 8 minutes. Beat in the Marsala, orange rind, and vanilla. Place the bowl or pot over hot water and heat, stirring constantly with a wooden spoon, making sure to reach the corners and bottom. Periodically coat the back of the spoon with the cream and draw your finger through it to test for thickness. When the line you have drawn remains intact, the custard is thick enough and should be removed from the heat. Pass it through a fine sieve to remove any lumps.

Allow the custard to cool for 10 minutes, stirring frequently, then cover and refrigerate until cold. To serve, whip the heavy cream until it holds a soft peak, then fold into the custard. Spoon into chilled wine glasses or custard cups and serve with fresh fruit, if desired. Zabaglione can be refrigerated for up to 2 hours before serving.

Serves 6. Preparation time: 45 minutes

 # CANNOLI

Cannoli are Sicilian pastries filled with a sweetened ricotta or, in this recipe, rum or chocolate pastry cream. To form the shells, use the special metal tubes 1-inch in diameter and 4-inches long which are available in baking supply stores and gourmet shops. Cannoli are best when fresh, but can be stored for a day. Fill them just before serving so that they are crisp and crunchy.

Pastry:

1 cup flour

1 tablespoon sugar

1 tablespoon cold butter, cut in pieces

¼ cup dry white wine

½ teaspoon cinammon

2 cups vegetable oil

1 recipe cold Pastry Cream (Page 180),
    rum or chocolate

¼ cup confectioners' sugar

2 tablespoons candied orange peel (optional)

Mound the flour on your work surface and make a well in the center. Place the sugar, butter, wine, and cinnamon in the well and gradually work in the flour. Form the dough into a ball and knead until smooth and elastic, about 8 minutes. Add a little flour if necessary to prevent sticking. Cover and refrigerate for at least 30 minutes.

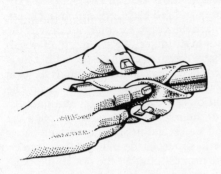

1 *Cut the pastry into circles about 4-inches in diameter and wrap around the cannoli tubes. Moisten and press together the overlapping edges to seal.*

2 *With a slotted spoon drop the cannoli into hot oil. Do not overcrowd the pan.*

3 *Gently turn to brown evenly on all sides, then remove and drain on paper towels. When cool, slide out the tube.*

4 *Pipe the cream into the cannoli using a pastry bag and working from each end.*

Pour the oil into a deep-fryer and slowly heat it to 375°, (see Page 12). Divide the dough into quarters and roll each to ⅟₁₆-inch thickness, either by hand or with a pasta machine. Using a cookie cutter, cut the pastry sheets into circles 4-inches in diameter. Wrap a circle of dough around a cannoli mold and moisten the overlapping edge with a little water; press the edges together where they meet. Continue to form the pastry around as many molds as you have. Carefully drop the pastry-molds into the hot fat, but do not overcrowd. Fry until golden brown on the first side, then turn them gently with a fork to cook the other side. Remove with a slotted spoon and drain on crumpled paper towels. When cool, the cannoli will slip from the molds, which can be washed and reused. Continue the process until all the dough has been used. (Leftover scraps of dough can be loosely knotted and fried to make Pastry Knots.)

To fill the cannoli, spoon the cold pastry cream into a pastry bag fitted with a large star tube. Pipe into the pastry shells, working from each end. Sprinkle with confectioners' sugar and garnish the ends with candied peel, if desired. Serve as soon as possible after filling.
Makes 8 cannoli. Preparation time: 1½ hours

PASTRY KNOTS
Cenci

Cenci are made from the same dough as cannoli, and are a good way to use any leftover pastry from that recipe.

1 recipe Cannoli dough (Page 182)

2 cups vegetable oil

½ cup confectioners' sugar

Prepare the dough according to the recipe for Cannoli. Allow it to rest, covered and refrigerated, for 30 minutes. Heat the oil to 375° in a deep-fryer (see method Page 12). Roll the dough to a ⅟₁₆-inch thickness and cut into irregular strips ½-inch by 8-inches. Tie the strips in loose knots. Carefully drop the knots into the hot fat, in batches to avoid overcrowding. Fry until golden brown, just several seconds, then gently turn and fry on the other side. Lift out with a slotted spoon and drain on crumpled paper towels. When cool, sift confectioners' sugar over them. Stored in an air-tight container, they will keep for 2 days.
Serves 6. Preparation time: 1 hour

GONFATI

I first sampled these delicious pastries at Il Drappo restaurant in Rome. They are crisp rounds of deep-fried dough filled with either a very mild goat cheese or with the mascarpone and pecorino mixture used here. The cheeses perfectly offset the sweetness of the fragrant honey, which can be heated to thin its consistency.

2 cups flour

½ teaspoon salt

1½ teaspoons baking powder

2 tablespoons sugar

1½ tablespoons cold vegetable shortening

½ cup milk, approximately

½ pound mascarpone or cream cheese, at
    room temperature

½ cup freshly grated pecorino romano

2 cups vegetable oil

1 cup honey

Combine the flour, salt, baking powder, and sugar, and sift into a bowl. Cut in the shortening and gradually add the milk while working it in with your fingertips. Work only until it holds together, then gather and knead the dough briefly, until it is smooth. Wrap the dough and refrigerate for at least 30 minutes.

While the dough is resting, make the filling. Cream the mascarpone or cream cheese and stir in the pecorino. Reserve.

Slowly heat the oil for deep-frying while rolling out the dough. Divide the dough in half and roll out to ⅛-inch thick on a lightly floured surface. Cut into 3-inch rounds. Place 1 teaspoon of the cheese in the center of each of half the rounds and brush the edges with milk or water. Gently top with another round (so that there will be a little air in the puffs) and crimp the edges together with the tines of a fork, about ¼-inch from the edge.

When the fat is hot (390°–400°), carefully drop the pastry into it, in batches. When the pastry is fried, it will blow up like a balloon. As soon as each rises to the surface, about 1 minute, turn it over to puff the other side. When the second side has browned, turn again to brown the first side. Remove with a slotted spoon and drain on paper towels. Transfer to a serving platter and drizzle with honey. Serve immediately.

Makes 12 to 15. Preparation time: 1¼ hours

ALMOND SPONGECAKE
Pan di Spagna con Mandorle

Though it's often called "Spanish Bread", this cake is a specialty of Genoa, where bake shops and home cooks all have their own versions. I like this one because it includes whole eggs and almonds. Eat it plain, frosted, or as a base for Zuppa Inglese (Page 201).

6 tablespoons butter, plus 1 teaspoon for pan

1 cup ground blanched almonds

1¼ cup sugar

4 eggs

2 tablespoons grappa or brandy

¾ cup flour

Confectioners' sugar (optional)

Preheat the oven to 400°. Butter an 8 or 9-inch springform pan. Line the bottom with parchment or wax paper and butter the paper. Melt the 6 tablespoons of butter and cool to lukewarm. Grind the nuts again, this time adding the sugar. Transfer to a mixing bowl (an electric mixer is best) and stir to break up any lumps. While beating the mixture, add the eggs one at a time, beating well after each addition. Beat in the grappa. The batter must be beaten for 10 minutes altogether, until it falls in a ribbon.

Carefully sift the flour over the top of the batter and gently fold it in with a rubber spatula. Drizzle in the melted butter, folding to catch it with the spatula before it falls to the bottom of the bowl. Fold the batter only until the butter is blended in; overmixing will deflate the eggs. Pour the batter into the prepared pan and bake for 10 minutes. Reduce the heat of the oven to 350° and continue to bake for 20 minutes, or until a toothpick inserted in the middle comes out clean. Remove from the oven and allow to cool in the pan. Release the springform sides and invert the cake onto a serving plate. Take off the pan bottom and paper. Dust with confectioners' sugar if desired.
Serves 6 to 8. Preparation time: 50 minutes

PEACH TART
Crostata di Pesche

Crostatas are flat tarts topped with a fine latticework, traditionally filled with fruit compotes and preserves. I prefer fresh, ripe fruits—plums, pears, and nectarines—in season, but good quality preserves can be substituted during winter months.

1 teaspoon butter
1 recipe Short Sweet Pastry (Page 179)
4 large ripe peaches
2 tablespoons lemon juice
¼ cup apricot preserves
½ egg, beaten

Preheat the oven to 400° and set a rack on the lowest setting. Butter a shallow 9-inch quiche pan or baking sheet. Divide the pastry in 2 pieces, making one portion twice as large as the other. Roll out the smaller portion between sheets of parchment or wax paper to a 6-inch by 10-inch rectangle. Place this in the freezer on a flat surface. Roll the larger portion of pastry to a 10-inch round and line the pan with it. If you're using a baking sheet, cut the dough into 9 to 10-inch round, using a plate as a guide to measuring and cutting it, then transfer to the baking sheet. Prick the dough with the tines of a fork and refrigerate.

To prepare the fruit, drop the peaches in boiling water for 20 seconds then refresh immediately in cold water. Peel and halve them. Cut into ¼-inch thick slices and toss with the lemon juice. Heat the apricot preserves over low heat until quite liquid, then strain through a sieve. Toss the peaches with the glaze, reserving 1 teaspoon to reglaze the baked tart.

Remove the pie crust from the refrigerator and top with the peaches, arranging them in flat concentric circles. Take the remaining pastry from the freezer, carefully peel off the top sheet of paper, and cut into ½-inch by 10-inch strips. To form the lattice top, lay strips in one direction 1-inch apart, then lay others diagonally across the pie in the opposite direction. Crimp the top and bottom crusts together. Brush the lattice with beaten egg. Place on the bottom rack of the oven and reduce the heat to 350°. Bake the pie for 30 minutes, until the crust is golden and the peaches tender. Remove from the oven and reglaze the peaches between the latticework. Serve warm, or make up to a day ahead and serve at room temperature.
Serves 6. Preparation time: 1 hour

GRAPE TART WITH ALMONDS
Crostata di Uva

Vary the proportions of green and red grapes as you wish, and if seed grapes are the only ones available, halve and pit them before using. If you prefer not to prebake the shell, bake the tart on the lowest rack of the oven. The tart will not brown on the bottom as nicely, but will bake in less time.

1 teaspoon butter

1 recipe Short Pastry (Page 178)

1 recipe Almond Pastry Cream (Page 181)

1 pound green seedless grapes

1 pound red seedless grapes

½ cup apricot preserves

½ cup slivered almonds, lightly toasted

Preheat the oven to 425°. Butter a 9-inch pie or quiche pan. Roll the pastry dough to ⅛-inch thickness and line the pan with it, fluting the edges. Prick the bottom with the tines of a fork and line with foil. Weight the foil with raw rice or dried beans, and prebake the pastry for 15 minutes, until it just begins to color. Remove from the oven, discard the foil and beans or rice, and allow the pastry to cool.

Make the pastry cream and pour it into the shell. Return to the oven, reduce the heat to 350° and bake for 30 minutes, until the cream is set and lightly browned. Remove the pie from the oven and cool slightly. Wash and clean the grapes, drain, and dry them on paper towels. Heat the apricot preserves over low heat until quite liquid, and strain through a sieve. Brush the top of the custard with about one third of the glaze. Arrange the grapes on the tart in a decorative pattern and brush them with the remaining glaze. Sprinkle the slivered almonds over the top.

Serves 6. Preparation time: 1 hour

CARAMELIZED ORANGES
Arance Caramelatte

6 large navel oranges
1½ cups water
3 cups sugar
2 tablespoons dark rum

Peel the oranges, then slice them into ¼-inch rounds and reconstruct them. Set them on a rack over a plate. Put the water in a heavy saucepan and add the sugar. Bring to a boil, swirling in the sugar until it dissolves. Boil until the sugar becomes thick and syrupy, about 5 minutes, then continue to cook until the sugar caramelizes and turns golden, another 5 to 8 minutes. Remove from the heat and, holding the pan at a distance, pour in the rum. Swirl it in, mixing with a clean spoon. Allow the caramel to cool and thicken slightly. Spoon the caramel over the oranges, so that it covers the tops and drips down the sides. Work quickly as the caramel will continue to harden (briefly return it to the heat and stir if it becomes too hard).

When all the oranges are glazed, allow them to harden for 10 minutes. To serve, snip off any excess caramel and arrange the fruit on dessert plates. Serve at once or reserve at room temperature—refrigeration will melt the caramel.
Serves 6. Preparation time: 30 minutes

PEACHES IN THE STYLE
OF PIEDMONT
Pesche alla Piemontese

In this recipe the peaches are lightly poached, then filled with a mixture that closely resembles the pits that have been removed.

12 macaroons (Page 172, or store-bought)
6 large ripe peaches
¼ cup lemon juice
3 cups dry white wine
1 cinnamon stick
2 cloves

¼ cup honey

1 tablespoon raspberry preserves

6 sprigs fresh mint

Preheat the oven to 350°. Crumble the macaroons and bake until browned and crisp, about 15 minutes. Remove and set aside. Drop the peaches into boiling water for 20 seconds, then refresh immediately in cold water. Peal the peaches and squeeze lemon juice over them to prevent discoloration.

Bring the wine to boil with the cinnamon, cloves, and honey in an oven-proof pan that can just hold the peaches. Add the peaches and bake for 15 minutes. If the peaches are not covered with liquid, turn them halfway through the poaching process. Remove from the oven and cool for 15 minutes, then refrigerate in the liquid for at least 30 minutes.

Shortly before serving, remove the peaches from the refrigerator. Halve along the natural crevice and pit. Mix together the macaroon crumbs and the raspberry preserves. Spoon a generous tablespoon of this mixture into the center of each peach, pressing it together so that it resembles the pit. Place the top half onto each peach bottom and secure with a toothpick. Garnish with fresh mint and serve.

Serves 6. Preparation time: 1¾ hours

PEARS STUFFED WITH GORGONZOLA AND HAZELNUTS
Pere al Gorgonzola

Pears are a refreshing fruit to serve with cheese, especially a blue-veined cheese such as gorgonzola. Toasted hazelnuts add crunch and flavor to the filling, which is hidden in the base of the cored pear and discovered when it is sliced open. Choose whichever pears are in season, and avoid any mushy or mealy fruit.

6 ripe pears

¼ cup lemon juice

6 ounces mascarpone, at room temperature

8 ounces crumbled gorgonzola, at room temperature

½ cup chopped toasted hazelnuts

Peel the pears (do not remove the stems) taking off as little of the fruit as possible and retaining the natural shape of the pear. Cut off the top portion of each pear at the bottom of the neck. Slice a little off the bottom of each pear so that it sits squarely on a plate. Scoop out the cores with a vegetable peeler or melon baller, making a cavity to hold about 2 tablespoons of filling. Rub the pears inside and out with the lemon juice.

Beat the mascarpone with a wooden spoon until smooth. Stir in the gorgonzola and nuts just until blended. Spoon 2 tablespoons of the cheese into each pear. Top the pears with the upper portions, matching the tops and bottoms. They can be kept for up to 1 hour at room temperature.

Serves 6. Preparation time: 15 minutes

 # RICOTTA AND HONEY PUDDING
Budino di Ricotta

Fresh Italian ricotta is sometimes served as dessert, sweetened with fresh fruit, sugar, or liqueur. In this recipe it is baked with eggs to produce a lighter pudding.

2 cups ricotta

2 tablespoons honey

4 eggs, separated

½ teaspoon vanilla

A pinch of salt

Cinammon to garnish

1 pint hulled fresh strawberries (optional)

Combine the ricotta, honey, egg yolks, and vanilla in the top of a double boiler over hot but not boiling water. Heat the mixture, stirring frequently, until hot to the touch. In a separate bowl, beat the egg whites with the salt until stiff but not dry. Pour the ricotta mixture into a bowl and fold in the beaten whites. Spoon the pudding into 6 wine glasses or pudding dishes. Sprinkle with cinnamon. Chill for up to 2 hours. Just before serving, garnish with strawberries.

Serves 6. Preparation time: 20 minutes

AMARETTO CARAMEL CUSTARD
Latte al'Amaretto

Here Amaretto liqueur is added to the custard in addition to the caramel for extra richness. Because of spattering, the liqueur should be added to the sugar slowly and at arm's length. The dessert can also be made in a large mold, but increase the baking time to 1 hour.

1¼ cups sugar

1 teaspoon lemon juice

½ cup water

2 tablespoons Amaretto

3 eggs

1 egg yolk

2 cups milk

½ teaspoon vanilla

Mix ¾ cup sugar, the lemon juice, and water in a heavy saucepan and bring to a boil, swirling the pan to dissolve the sugar. Cook until it is golden in color, about 5 minutes, swirling the pan from time to time. Add 1 tablespoon of Amaretto, swirling it into the caramel, then pour the mixture into six ½–¾ cup ramekins or oven-proof serving cups; set aside.

Preheat the oven to 300°. In a mixing bowl, beat the eggs, the egg yolk, and the remaining sugar together. Whisk in the milk, vanilla, and remaining Amaretto. Strain the egg mixture into the ramekins on top of the caramel. Place in a baking pan and fill with enough hot water to come halfway up the sides of the ramekins. Bake for 30 minutes, until they are set and a knife inserted in the center comes out clean. Remove from the oven and allow to cool in the water bath. The custards can be served warm or refrigerated until cold. To unmold, run a sharp knife around the inside of the molds and invert.
Serves 6. Preparation time: 1 hour

CARAMELIZED RICE CAKE
Torta di Riso Caramellato

A specialty of Bologna, this cake's long slow cooking of rice in milk is reminiscent of rice pudding. Arborio rice turns slightly brown, and the caramel covers the top with a rich amber glaze. The cake is delicious served warm.

1 quart milk
½ teaspoon vanilla
1 tablespoon dark rum
¼ teaspoon salt
⅓ cup rice, preferably Arborio
2 cups sugar
½ cup water
1 teaspoon lemon juice
⅓ cup sultana raisins
⅓ cup dark raisins
5 eggs, lightly beaten

In a heavy saucepan, bring the milk to a boil, but do not allow it to boil over. Stir in the vanilla, rum, salt, rice, and 1 cup of the sugar. Reduce the heat to a low simmer and cook the rice, partially covered, for 2 hours, stirring occasionally.

Put the remaining cup of sugar in a heavy saucepan and mix in the water and lemon juice. Do not stir but bring to a boil, swirling the pan until the sugar is dissolved, and cook until the sugar caramelizes and is golden, about 5 minutes. Immediately pour the caramel into a 6 to 8-cup mold and tilt the mold back and forth to cover the bottom evenly; set aside.

When the rice has cooked for 2 hours, stir in the raisins and continue simmering, stirring frequently, for 30 minutes more, until the rice is mushy and sticks to the bottom of the pan. Remove from the heat and cool slightly.

Preheat the oven to 325°. Whisk the eggs into the rice and pour into the prepared mold. Place the mold in a baking pan and add enough hot water to come halfway up the outside of the mold. Bake the torta for 1 hour, until the custard is set and a knife inserted in the center comes out clean. Remove from the oven and allow to set for 10 minutes. Run a sharp knife around the sides of the mold and invert the cake onto a serving platter. To store, refrigerate the torta in the mold.
Serves 6. Preparation time: 3¾ hours

CANDIED ORANGE AND LEMON PEEL
Scorza di Arancia e Limone Candita

Many traditional Italian desserts call for glacéed fruits: citron, angelica, and cherries. Although this was a good way of preserving fruits before refrigeration, they are often heavy and stale. When freshly made, the orange and lemon peels are cooked to a shiny transparency and retain a tartness which is nicely balanced by the sugar.

2 large oranges and/or 3 large lemons (2 cups peel)

2 cups water

1½ cups sugar

1 tablespoon lemon juice

Wash the fruits in warm water and dry with a clean towel. Slit the skins from the stem end to the base around the fruit so that the rind is halved, then quartered. Pry away the skin with a knife and peel off the 4 sections. Thinly slice the peel into strips ⅛-inch wide and 1½ to 2-inches long. Blanch the peel in boiling water for 10 minutes and drain, removing any white pith; set aside.

Pour the water into a small heavy saucepan and add the sugar and lemon juice. Bring the mixture to a boil, swirling the pan to dissolve the sugar. Add the citrus peel and simmer uncovered for 2 hours, stirring occasionally. Cover the pot, remove from the heat and allow the peel to steep in the sugar syrup for 12 hours. Drain the peel on a rack over a pan to catch the drippings. Allow 12 hours for draining and drying. Candied fruit can be covered and stored in the refrigerator for up to 3 months.

Makes 2 cups. Preparation time (not including soaking and draining): 2¼ hours

CHEESECAKE
Torta di Formaggio

Richer and creamier than a traditional Italian cheesecake, this torta, which can be topped with a lemon curd, is quite large, but none of it will go to waste.

Cheesecake:

1 teaspoon butter

1 recipe Sweet Short Pastry (Page 179)

1 pound cream cheese, at room temperature

2 cups ricotta, at room temperature

¾ cup sugar

1 teaspoon vanilla

6 eggs

1 tablespoon sifted cornstarch

1 cup sour cream

½ cup Candied Lemon Peel (Page 194) or
    citron, in small dice

Topping: (Optional)

½ cup butter

1 cup sugar

2 tablespoons grated lemon rind

⅓ cup lemon juice

A pinch of salt

2 eggs

Butter a 9-inch springform pan. Roll out the sweet pastry and line the bottom of the pan. Cut the leftover pieces to line the sides of the pan, pressing and molding together to form a smooth crust. Refrigerate until the filling is prepared.

Preheat the oven to 325°. In a mixing bowl, beat the cream cheese until smooth and light (use the paddle attachment if your mixer has one). Add the ricotta and blend well, scraping the sides of the bowl. Add the sugar and vanilla, then beat in the eggs one at a time, mixing well after each addition. Add the cornstarch, sour cream, and lemon peel, scraping the bowl and blending well. Pour the filling into the prepared pan and bake for 1½ hours. Loosely cover the top of the cake with foil if it begins to brown. Remove from the oven and allow to cool completely before removing the springform.

When the cake is nearly cool, make the lemon curd. Melt the butter in a small, heavy saucepan or the top of a double boiler over simmering water. Stir in the sugar, lemon rind and juice, and salt. Remove from the heat. Beat the eggs until light and whisk in the lemon-butter mixture. Pour this into the pan and set over medium heat or simmering water. Stir constantly with a wooden spoon until the curd thickens, about 8 minutes, but do not allow it to boil. Pour into a clean bowl and let cool. When the cheesecake is cool, remove it from the springform, pour the topping into the center of the cake and spread evenly with a long knife or metal spatula. Refrigerate the cake until ready to serve.
Serves 12. Preparation time: 2½ hours

CHILLED FRUIT SALAD
Macedonia di Frutta

Maraschino is a sweet liqueur made from cherries, and adds a sparkle to this salad. Vary the fruits for season—fresh figs, berries, or peaches are good additions.

2 oranges

2 ripe pears

3 tablespoons lemon juice

2 red apples

2 bananas

1 cup fresh-squeezed orange juice

2 teaspoons grated lemon rind

2 tablespoons maraschino liqueur

Using a sharp knife, peel and section the oranges. Peel and core the pear and cut into bite-size pieces. Toss with the lemon juice. Core the unpeeled apples, cut into bite-size pieces and toss with the pears. Peel the banana and slice, toss with the pears and apples, then toss in the oranges. Add the orange juice, lemon rind, and liqueur, and toss well. Chill until ready to serve. Spoon into compotes or long-stemmed wine glasses.
Serves 6. Preparation time: 20 minutes

PEARS POACHED IN RED WINE
Pere in Chianti

As they poach, the pears take on the ruby red color of the wine. Ripe pears are the most flavorful, but if the pears are a little hard, increase the cooking time.

4 cups chianti
1¾ cups sugar
1 teaspoon black peppercorns
2 bay leaves
2 2-inch strips lemon peel
6 ripe, unblemished pears
¼ cup lemon juice

Using a saucepan in which the pears will fit standing closely together, bring the wine to a boil with the sugar, peppercorns, bay leaves, and lemon peel. Reduce the heat to simmer. Meanwhile, peel the pears but do not remove the stems. Try to take off as little of the skin as possible and keep the natural shape of the pear. Rub the pears with lemon juice. Carefully set the pears upright in the wine mixture and adjust the heat so that it barely simmers. Cook for 15 to 30 minutes, until a toothpick inserted meets with just a little resistance. Remove the pears and set aside. Bring the poaching liquid to a boil. Strain and reduce the liquid to a thick, syrupy glaze that coats the back of a spoon, about 5 minutes. Cool the sauce, then spoon some of it over the pears. To serve, place one pear in the middle of each of 6 dessert plates and spoon the remaining sauce on top.
Serves 6. Preparation time: 1½ hours

RICH CHOCOLATE CAKE
Torta di Cioccolata

This is a very rich cake and may seem a bit complicated, but for chocolate-lovers it's well worth the effort. Garnish the cake's shiny glaze with *croccante,* an Italian praline.

Cake:

3 cups blanched almonds

12 ounces bittersweet chocolate, in pieces

1½ cups butter, plus 1 teaspoon for pan, at room
    temperature

1½ cups sugar

6 eggs, separated, at room temperature

1 teaspoon vanilla

¼ teaspoon salt

Filling:

½ recipe Pastry Cream (Page 180), made with 3
    ounces of bittersweet chocolate

Glaze:

8 ounces bittersweet chocolate

3 tablespoons espresso coffee, or 1 tablespoon instant
    espresso dissolved in 3 tablespoons boiling water

¼ cup butter

½ teaspoon vanilla

Praline:

1 teaspoon butter

½ cup water

1 cup sugar

¾ cup whole blanched almonds, lightly toasted

Preheat the oven to 300°. Butter a 9-inch springform pan and set aside. Finely chop the almonds by hand, in a blender, or in a food processor. Add the chocolate and chop together until they are finely ground. In a large bowl, cream the butter and gradually add 1 cup of sugar. Beat until light and fluffy, then add the egg yolks one at a time, blending well after each addition. Beat in the salt, vanilla, and chocolate mixture, mixing until the batter is smooth. In a clean bowl, beat the egg whites until light and slightly stiff. Whip in the remaining ½ cup of sugar gradually and continue to beat until soft peaks form. Fold one-quarter of the whites into the chocolate batter, which should be quite thick. When these have been evenly distributed, fold in the remaining whites and pour into the prepared pan. Bake for 1 hour, until a toothpick inserted in the center comes out clean. Allow the cake to cool in the pan.

As the cake cools, prepare the pastry cream, glaze, and praline. To make the glaze, put the chocolate and espresso in a heavy saucepan over medium heat or in the top of a double boiler over simmering water. Stir constantly until the chocolate is melted and the mixture smooth. Remove from the heat and add the butter, stirring until it has melted. Add the vanilla and set aside to cool to room temperature, stirring occasionally. Butter a baking sheet for the praline. Put the water in a heavy saucepan and add the sugar. Over medium heat bring the mixture to a boil, swirling the pan from time to time to dissolve the sugar, but do not stir. The sugar will thicken and caramelize, turning a golden color. This will take several minutes. Add the almonds and stir to coat them evenly with sugar syrup. Continue to cook until the caramel is a deep amber, then pour out onto the prepared baking sheet. Quickly spread the brittle with a metal spoon and allow to cool. Coarsely chop the praline with a sharp knife so that several shiny chunks remain.

Unmold the springform and invert the cake into a rack. Slide the springform bottom under the cake to make it easier to handle. Carefully slice the cake into 2 layers with a long, serrated knife and remove the top layer. Mix the chocolate pastry cream with half the praline, saving the most attractive chunks to decorate the cake. Spread all the cream on the bottom layer. Replace the top layer.

Stir the glaze until smooth. Place the cake on a rack over a plate and pour the glaze over it, spreading with a spatula so that it coats the cake evenly on the top and around the sides. (The glaze that drips onto the plate can be reheated and used to fill in any gaps.) When the glaze is somewhat firm, transfer the cake (on the springform bottom) to a serving plate. Arrange the reserved praline chunks around the bottom edges or on top of the cake. Refrigerate for at least 30 minutes before serving, but if the cake is very cold allow it to sit at room temperature for 1 hour before serving.

Serves 12. Preparation time: 2¼ hours

CHESTNUT MOUNTAIN
Monte Bianco

This is an autumn and winter dessert molded to resemble the snow-covered peak of Monte Bianco, which straddles the Italian, Swiss, and French borders. I have used canned chestnuts but you can substitute 2 pounds of fresh ones, adding more milk or water if necessary.

1 16-ounce can chestnuts

3 cups milk

A pinch of salt

1 teaspoon vanilla

1 ounce bittersweet chocolate, chopped

½ cup water

½ cup sugar

6 egg whites

1 cup heavy cream

Simmer the chestnuts in their liquid with the milk, salt, and vanilla over low heat, stirring frequently, until the mixture thickens, about 45 minutes. (The consistency should not be as thick as mashed potatoes but retain its shape when stirred.) Remove from the heat and stir in the chocolate until it has melted. Purée the chestnuts in the food processor or by passing through a food mill or sieve.

Pour ½ cup of water into a heavy saucepan and add the sugar. Bring to a boil, swirling the pan to dissolve the sugar, but do not stir. Cook the sugar to the soft ball stage (238°–240°), when a little of the syrup dropped into cold water forms a soft ball. This will take about 5 minutes. The syrup will thicken and the boiling bubbles become larger as it reaches this stage. While the syrup is cooking, beat the egg whites in a large bowl until stiff but not dry. When the syrup is ready, gradually pour it into the whites in a thin stream while continuing to beat. Beat until the mixture is cool and soft peaks form.

Meanwhile, beat the chestnuts with a wooden spoon or rework in the food processor; transfer to a large bowl. Fold the whites into the chestnuts, one quarter at a time to lighten the mixture. Fit a pastry bag with a large star tube and spoon the mixture into it. Pipe onto a serving platter in a circular motion, forming a cone shape, moving the bag around and up, making narrower circles each time, so that it gives the impression of a mountain. Set aside in a cool place.

Just before serving, beat the heavy cream until soft peaks form. Spoon some of the cream on top of the 'mountain' to resemble snow.

Serve immediately, passing the extra whipped cream separately.
Serves 6. Preparation time: 1½ hours

 ## ZUPPA INGLESE

This version of the English trifle is made with spongecake flavored with hazelnuts and cherries, spiked with a cherry liqueur, and layered with a rich custard.

Hazelnut Cake:

1 teaspoon butter

6 eggs, separated, at room temperature

⅔ cup sugar

½ teaspoon vanilla

½ cup finely chopped, toasted, peeled hazelnuts

¼ cup flour

¼ cup cherry liqueur, preferably Peter Heering

1 16-ounce can sour cherries in water, well-drained
   and pitted

Pastry Cream:

2 cups milk

6 egg yolks

¼ cup sugar

1 teaspoon vanilla

2 tablespoons flour

Preheat the oven to 350°. Butter an 8-inch springform pan and set aside. In a large mixing bowl, beat the egg yolks with ⅓ cup of sugar and the vanilla until lemon-colored and glossy, about 5 minutes. In a separate bowl with clean beaters, beat the egg whites until stiff but not dry. While beating, gradually add the remaining ⅓ cup of sugar and continue to beat until stiff. Place the whites on top of the yolk mixture, sprinkle the nuts on them, and sift the flour over all. Gently fold all of these ingredients together. Pour the batter into the pan and bake for 30 minutes, until lightly browned and springy to the touch.

Allow the cake to rest for 10 minutes, then unmold it onto a rack and let cool completely. Trim away the browned crust at the sides of the cake, then carefully slice it into four layers. Place the bottom layer browned side up in the bottom of a large serving bowl, preferably glass. Brush with liqueur and top with one quarter of the pitted sour cherries. Set aside.

To make the pastry cream, bring the milk to a boil in a medium saucepan, being careful not to let it boil over. Cover and remove from the heat. In a separate bowl, beat the yolks while gradually adding the sugar and vanilla. Sift the flour over the yolks and whisk it in. Gradually pour the hot milk into the yolks, then return the mixture to the saucepan. Over medium heat, cook the cream, stirring constantly, until it is thick. Pour one quarter of the cream over the prepared cake and cherries. Cover with the top of cake, browned side up. Brush with liqueur and top with one quarter of the cherries. Pour over another quarter of the cream. Repeat the process with the remaining two layers, saving the last of the cherries to decorate the top. Serve immediately or cool and refrigerate until ready to serve.

Serves 6. Preparation time: 1 1/4 hours

CHAPTER 13

ICES

W ith good reason, Italy is renowned for its fresh ices which can range from smooth sherbets to the coarser-grained granita to rich ice creams. Unlike many of our poor imitations, they are flavored with fresh fruit syrups, coffee, chocolate, and liqueurs and studded with candied fruit or nuts. Although water ices are sometimes served as a palate cleanser during a meal, sherbets are normally eaten in bars or cafes with an espresso or a liqueur as a refreshing break towards the end of a hot day.

Fortunately for us, the nature of granita and sherbet means that they can be made at home in the freezer (as indeed can the two ice creams in this chapter). However, an electric ice cream machine will, of course, make the procedure much easier (see page 13).

A good fresh ice should be not too sweet, but rather light and smooth in consistency and just cold enough to melt in your mouth without giving that uncomfortable tingling sensation that shows it has been frozen too hard. When making it by hand it is a little harder to control the final consistency, so do check it regularly as it hardens in the freezer. Of course, the length of time for freezing will depend on the efficiency of your freezer but with a little experience using the times I have given as guidelines you will be able to control your results more accurately.

Fresh ices are traditionally associated with Naples and Sicily and many of the most popular and richest ice creams are based on a Sicilian specialty— zabaglione. These ice creams are served plain or flavored, sometimes sprinkled with fresh strawberries, cherries, or other fruit, or studded with chopped nuts or a colorful mixture of fresh candied peel.

BANANA SHERBET
Sorbetto di Banana

Buy bananas a few days ahead ... the fruit should be unbruised and just beginning to develop the little brown spots that tell you the bananas are becoming soft and over-ripe.

1½ cups mashed banana (about 3 medium bananas)
¼ cup sugar
3 tablespoons lemon juice
1¼ cups water
Fresh mint for garnish

Place the bananas, sugar, and lemon juice in a blender or food processor and blend until smooth. Or pass the fruit mixed with the lemon juice and sugar through a food mill or sieve. Gradually add the water while blending until the mixture is light and fluffy. Freeze in an ice cream machine, following the manufacturer's instructions for sherbet.

If you do not have a machine, pour the mixture into very clean ice cube trays or a metal bowl. Freeze for 45 to 60 minutes, until the mixture begins to get mushy and solidify, then beat the sorbetto with a fork while still in the freezer, scraping the crystals from the sides of the container. This gives the sherbet a fluffier texture and keeps it from freezing into a solid block. Whisk at 30 minute intervals for up to 3 hours, using a spoon as the sherbet hardens. When the consistency is firm but beatable (not frozen solid) the sorbetto is ready to serve. Beat once again and spoon into chilled wine glasses or bowls; garnish with mint.

Serves 6. Preparation time: Up to 3¼ hours

ORANGE AND LEMON SHERBET
Sorbetto Siciliano

The zest of citrus fruits contains the most concentrated flavor, while the white pith below is bitter and should not be used. A special zester or a vegetable peeler with a sharp blade is helpful to remove the colored peel.

1¼ cups orange juice

¾ cup tangerine juice

½ cup lemon juice

1 tablespoon orange zest, in fine julienne

1 tablespoon lemon zest, in fine julienne

2 teaspoons tangerine zest, in fine julienne

1 cup water

⅓ cup sugar

6 thin orange slices, for garnish

Fresh mint for garnish

Squeeze and strain the juices; reserve. Combine the zests with water and sugar in a heavy saucepan. Bring to a simmer, stirring often with a whisk, until the sugar dissolves. Allow to cool. Strain this liquid into the fruit juices and discard the zest. Chill for at least 1 hour, then follow the freezing directions for Banana Sherbet, opposite.

Serves 6. Preparation time: Up to 3¼ hours

STRAWBERRY SHERBET
Sorbetto di Fragole

2 pints ripe strawberries, hulled

3 tablespoons fresh-squeezed orange juice

3 tablespoons lemon juice

½ cup sugar

1½ cups water

Fresh mint for garnish

Reserve 6 whole strawberries for garnish and purée the rest in a blender, food processor, food mill, or by passing through a sieve. Mix with the citrus juices, sugar, and water. Freeze in an ice-cream machine according to the manufacturer's instructions for sherbet or following the method for Banana Sherbet, Page 204.

Spoon the sherbet into chilled wine glasses and garnish with a strawberry and fresh mint.

Serves 6. Preparation time: up to 3¼ hours

 ## ESPRESSO ICE
Granita Espresso

The rich coffee flavor of espresso is captured in this granita. Make the espresso with double-roasted, freshly ground beans, using 3 times as much coffee as you normally would. You do not need an ice cream machine to make this dessert. In fact, the texture of machine-made sherbet is too smooth to be labelled a granita. It is important that flakes of ice form and are gently mixed in; when served, the granita will resemble translucent mica. Add lightly sweetened whipped cream to make cappuccino ice.

3 cups strong freshly brewed espresso, or

    6 tablespoons instant espresso dissolved in

    3 cups boiling water

6 tablespoons sugar

6 twists lemon peel

Mix the hot coffee with the sugar and refrigerate until cool. Pour into very clean ice trays or bread pans, or any non-plastic bowl, to a depth of 1-inch or less and place in the freezer. After 1 hour, ice crystals should begin forming around the edges. Gently stir the granita to mix the crystals into the liquid. Freeze for about 3 hours, stirring the granita every 30 minutes, until the consistency is flaky but thoroughly iced. Serve within 30 minutes, spooning into chilled wine glasses and garnishing each with a twist of lemon peel.

Serves 6. Preparation time: 3¼ hours

 # SAMBUCA SHERBET
Sorbetto di Sambuca

Sambuca is usually sipped as an after dinner drink with a coffee bean floating in it to cut its sweetness. The liqueur makes a refreshing sherbet which can be served between courses to cleanse the palate.

3 cups water
2 cups sugar
½ cup Sambuca or anisette liqueur
¼ cup lemon juice
2 tablespoons lime juice

Place 2 cups of water in a heavy saucepan and add the sugar. Bring to a boil, swirling the pan from time to time to dissolve the sugar. When it boils, pour the syrup into a heat-proof container and add the liqueur, lemon and lime juices, and remaining 1 cup of water. Refrigerate until cool. Freeze the sherbet according to the directions for Banana Sherbet, Page 204, or the manufacturer's instructions for your ice cream machine. (As the alcohol raises the freezing temperature of the mixture, the sorbetto may take a little longer to freeze than fruit sherbets.) Serve in chilled glasses.

Serves 6. Preparation time: Up to 4 hours

 # ZABAGLIONE ICE CREAM
Gelato di Zabaglione

The richest ice creams are made from a custard similar to zabaione, which must be cooked and cooled before freezing. The advance planning, though, is well worth it.

6 egg yolks

¾ cup sugar

1 cup Marsala

Grated rind of 1 large orange

1 tablespoon vanilla

2 cups heavy cream

In a small, heavy saucepan or the top of a double boiler, beat the egg yolks and sugar until lemon-colored and glossy, about 5 minutes. Whisk in the Marsala, orange rind, and vanilla. Stir the mixture constantly with a wooden spoon over medium heat or simmering water until it thickens. (It should coat the back of a spoon and hold a line drawn through it with your finger.) Immediately remove from the heat and strain the sauce into a bowl. Refrigerate until cool.

Stir in the heavy cream, then make the ice cream according to the directions for Banana Sherbet on Page 204 or the manufacturer's instructions for your ice cream maker. Serve in chilled, long-stemmed glasses or bowls.

Serves 6. Preparation time: Up to 3½ hours

MOCHA ICE CREAM
Gelato di Mocha

6 egg yolks

¾ cup sugar

2 cups milk

¼ cup strong, freshly brewed espresso, or 1 tablespoon
   instant espresso dissolved in ¼ cup boiling water

½ teapsoon vanilla

12 ounces bittersweet chocolate, coarsely chopped

2 cups heavy cream

Follow the directions for Zabaglione Ice Cream (Page 207), adding the milk and espresso to the eggs and sugar. Whisk in the vanilla, stir until thickened, then strain into a bowl. Add the coarsely chopped chocolate and stir in until melted. Refrigerate until cool, then stir in the heavy cream and follow the freezing directions for Banana Sherbet, Page 204.

Serves 6. Preparation time: Up to 3¼ hours

Some Italian Cheeses

Asiago is a semi-firm or grana type cheese from Veneto. At its youngest, *asiago grasso di monte* is a smooth and slightly sweet asiago which is served as an eating cheese. The aged *asiago d'allevio* is more widely available and is a sharp grating cheese.

Bel Paese is a factory-made semi-soft eating cheese from Lombardy (the name means "beautiful country", and genuine imported bel paese has a map of Italy on its wrapper.) A slightly sweet cow's milk cheese, it has fairly good melting qualities.

Caciocavallo or "horse cheese", is so-called because two pear-shaped cheeses are often tied together to resemble saddlebags. This smooth, white eating cheese is similar in taste and texture to mozzarella, becoming sharper and firmer with age.

Fontina is a cooking and eating cheese from the Valle d'Aosta and is used primarily in the North, where its fine melting capability is exploited in fonduta. A yellowish, semi-hard cheese, with small holes scattered throughout, fontina has a delicate, nutty flavor. Danish fontina is often more available in this country but does not have the flavor of the Italian product.

Gorgonzola is a blue-veined eating cheese sometimes used in cooking, most often compared with French Roquefort. Until recently, most gorgonzolas were the pungent, aged variety, but some stores now also carry a younger gorgonzola which is a sweeter, creamier variety that may appeal to those who prefer their cheeses less assertive.

Groviera Italiano is Italian gruyere, made in the Lombardy region near the Swiss border. It is a pale yellow, mild, slightly sweet eating and cooking cheese which may be substituted with Swiss or French gruyere or emmenthal.

Mascarpone is a fresh, mild, triple-cream cheese made during the winter, in Lombardy. Sold in 4-ounce portions in muslin bags, it is often eaten as a dessert, rather like cream cheese which it resembles, with fruit or sprinkled with sugar. It is also used to make torte, layered with other cheeses such as gorgonzola, and herbs, fruit, or nuts.

Mozzarella was traditionally made in the South of Italy from buffalo milk, but most of the production is now made from cow's milk. *Mozzarella di bufalo* can be found in some specialty cheese shops, it may only be made from 30 percent buffalo milk but it will still have a more gamey flavor than the cow's milk version.

Most mozzarella is sold prepackaged, but it is softer and less rubbery when bought fresh, swimming in a bowl of whey or brine, from an Italian grocery store. Grated mozzarella melts very well and is the classic topping for pizzas. However, many prefer it sliced with a little black pepper and olive oil and perhaps fresh tomatoes and basil. Smoked mozzarella is particularly delicious served this way.

Parmigiano Reggiano or Parmesan, is the foremost grana cooking cheese of Italy, contributing its rich, tangy flavor to countless dishes and nearly every meal with pasta. True parmesan is made and marketed in Parma and neighboring Reggio-Emilia and has a brown rind stamped with the name Parmigiano Reggiano. Parmesan is aged for two, three, or four or more years, producing vecchio (old), stravecchio (older), and stravecchione (oldest) cheeses respectively, and increasing in flavor and hardness with age. The younger, moister parmesan is an excellent dessert cheese.

For optimal freshness and flavor, parmesan should be grated as you need it, even passing the cheese and grater at the table. The hard rind may be added to soups or stewed légumes to impart a spicy, almost salty flavor to the dish, and removed just before serving. American and Argentine parmesan cheeses are not equal to the original Italian cheese.

Pecorino is ewe's milk cheese, of which there are many varieties in Italy. The most widely available in the United States is the aged *pecorino romano,* which is used for grating and cooking in a similar way to parmesan. *Pecorino sardo,* from Sardinia, is a white cheese with a black paraffin coating and a sharp, salty flavor.

Provolone is often seen hanging by string in round or pear shapes in Italian groceries, or in fanciful shapes such as pigs and elephants. Although there are young and smoked eating provolones, most of what you see is the semi-hard, pale, tangy cooking cheese. Michigan and Wisconsin produce American versions of provolone; these tend not to be as flavorful as the Italian product.

Ricotta is made from the leftover whey from other cheeses to produce a mild, white, soft curd cheese. The traditional ingredient in lasagne, manicotti, and other stuffed pastas, this creamy cheese can even be eaten sprinkled with olive oil, salt, and freshly ground pepper for a simple lunch, or with sugar for dessert.

The part-skim variety sold in the supermarkets is drier and closer to the Italian original. If the cheese seems watery, place it in a cheesecloth-lined sieve to drain for a few hours before using. *Ricotta salata,* made in the south of Italy, is salted and dried, and can be grated and used in cooking or salads. Generally, it can be found in Italian groceries.

Scarmorze was originally an Abruzzi specialty made from buffalo milk. The shepherds of the region would roast the cheese over an open fire until creamy and spread it warm on bread. It is now produced in other regions with cow's and goat's milk in addition to, or replacing buffalo. Somewhat similar to mozzarella, it comes in ball or pear shapes and varying degrees of hardness; the best are dry on the outside but still semi-soft inside.

Taleggio is a semi-soft, fragrant cheese from the Lombardy, which makes a deliciously piquant after-dinner cheese. The cheese is square with an orange rind and when over-ripe will smell ammoniated.

Torte are not a cheese but usually two different soft Italian cheeses layered with herbs (often basil), nuts (pine nuts or walnuts), or fruit. The combinations will offset each other in the best examples, in the worst the characters of the cheeses and flavorings compete to create an unpleasant mixture of tastes. However, a good torta is an excellent dessert cheese.

INDEX

Bibliography:

Buglialli, Guillano, *Classic Techniques of Italian Cooking* (Simon & Schuster) and *The Fine Art of Italian Cooking* (Times Books)

Hazan, Marcella, *The Classic Italian Cookbook* and *More Italian Cooking* (Alfred A. Knopf)

Hazelton, Nika, *Regional Italian Cooking* (Evans)

Romagnoli, Margaret & G. Franco, *Italian Family Recipes From the Romagnolis' Table* (Atlantic-Little, Brown)

Root, Waverly, *The Food of Italy* (Random House)

Simac, *The Joy of Pasta* (Simac Appliances Corporation)

Acknowledgments:

Smallwood & Stewart wish to thank Rosina De Luca Kagel, who provided invaluable help and guidance in the early stages of this book.

Illustrations by Ed Lipinski.

The authors wish to thank Harriet Reilly and Theresa Lombardi Magistro for recipe ideas and testing; Mario Cardullo, the Renaissance Chef, for valuable historical information; and The Simac Appliances Corporation, for the use of an electric pasta maker and ice cream machine.